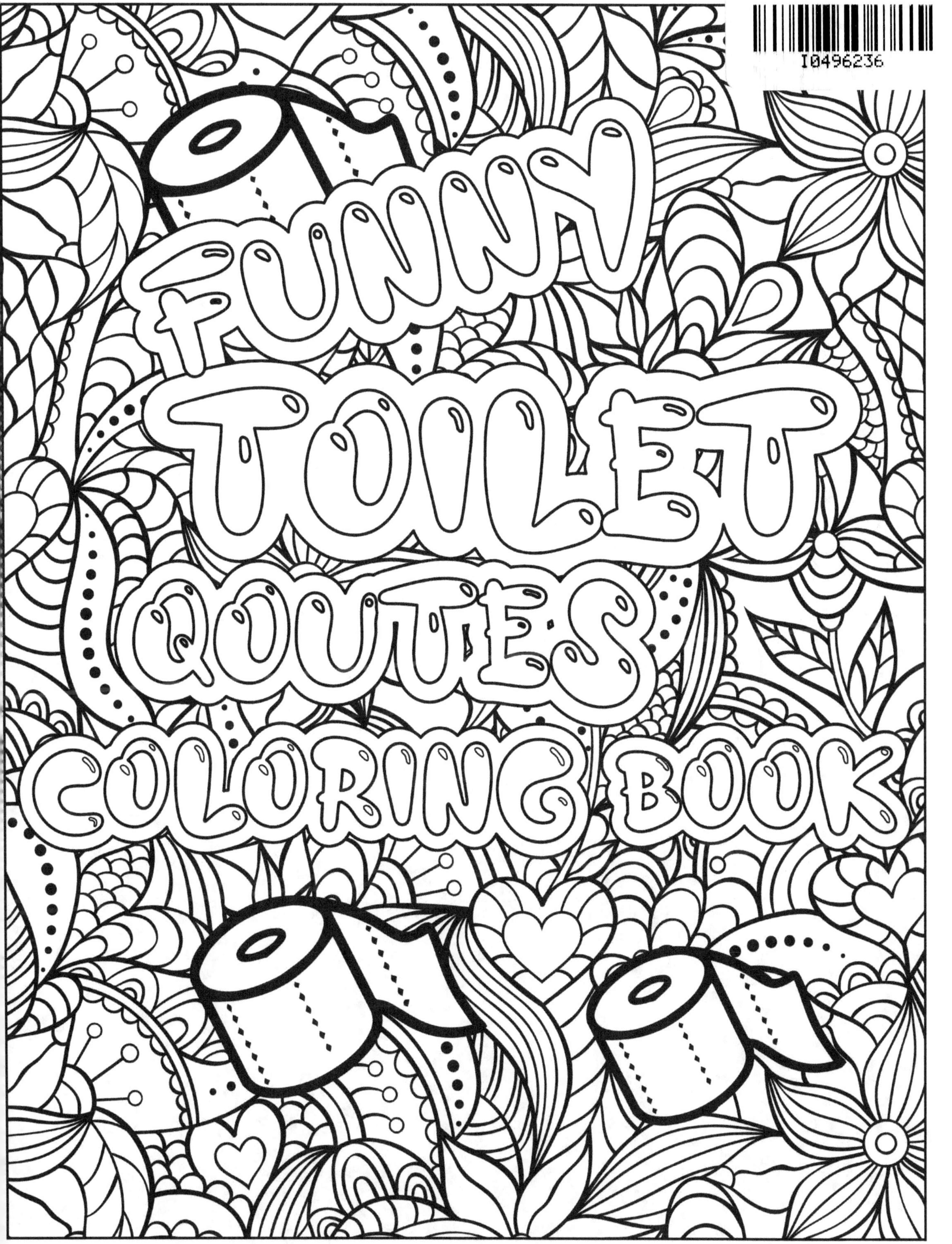
FUNNY
TOILET
QOUTES
COLORING BOOK

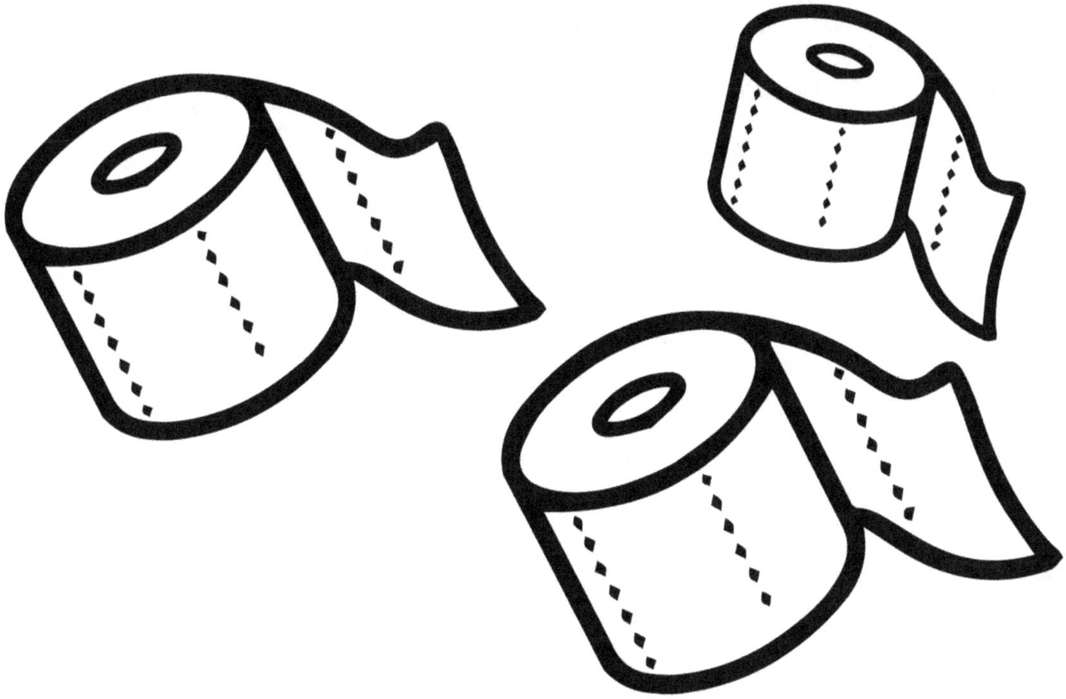

THIS BOOK BELONGS TO:

____

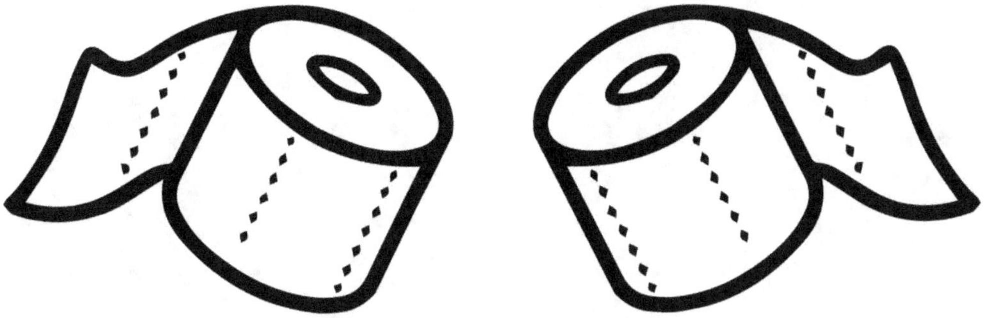

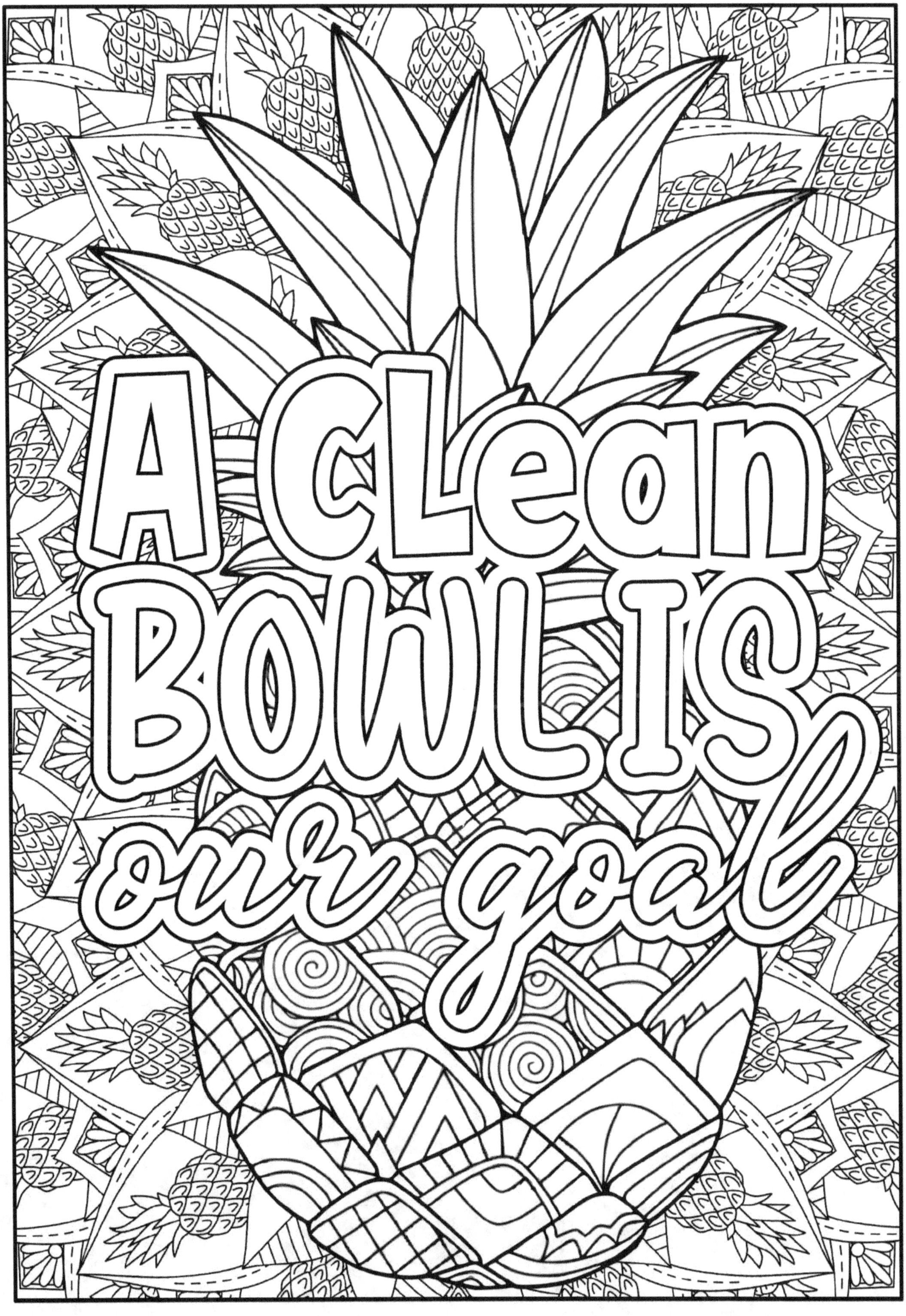
A CLean
BOWL IS
our goal

CHANGING THE TOILET
PAPER WILL NOT
CAUSE BRAIN
Damage

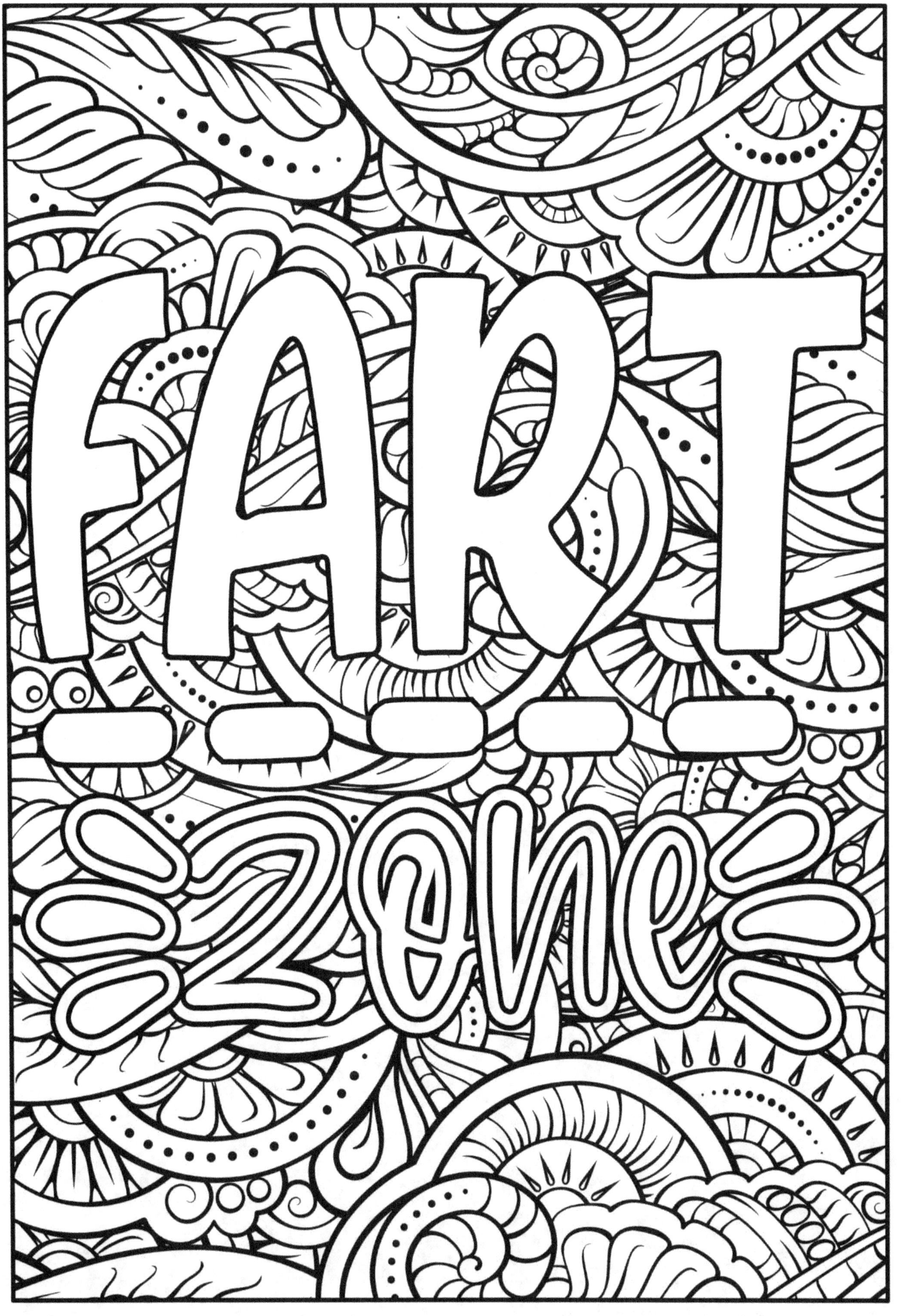
FART
Zone

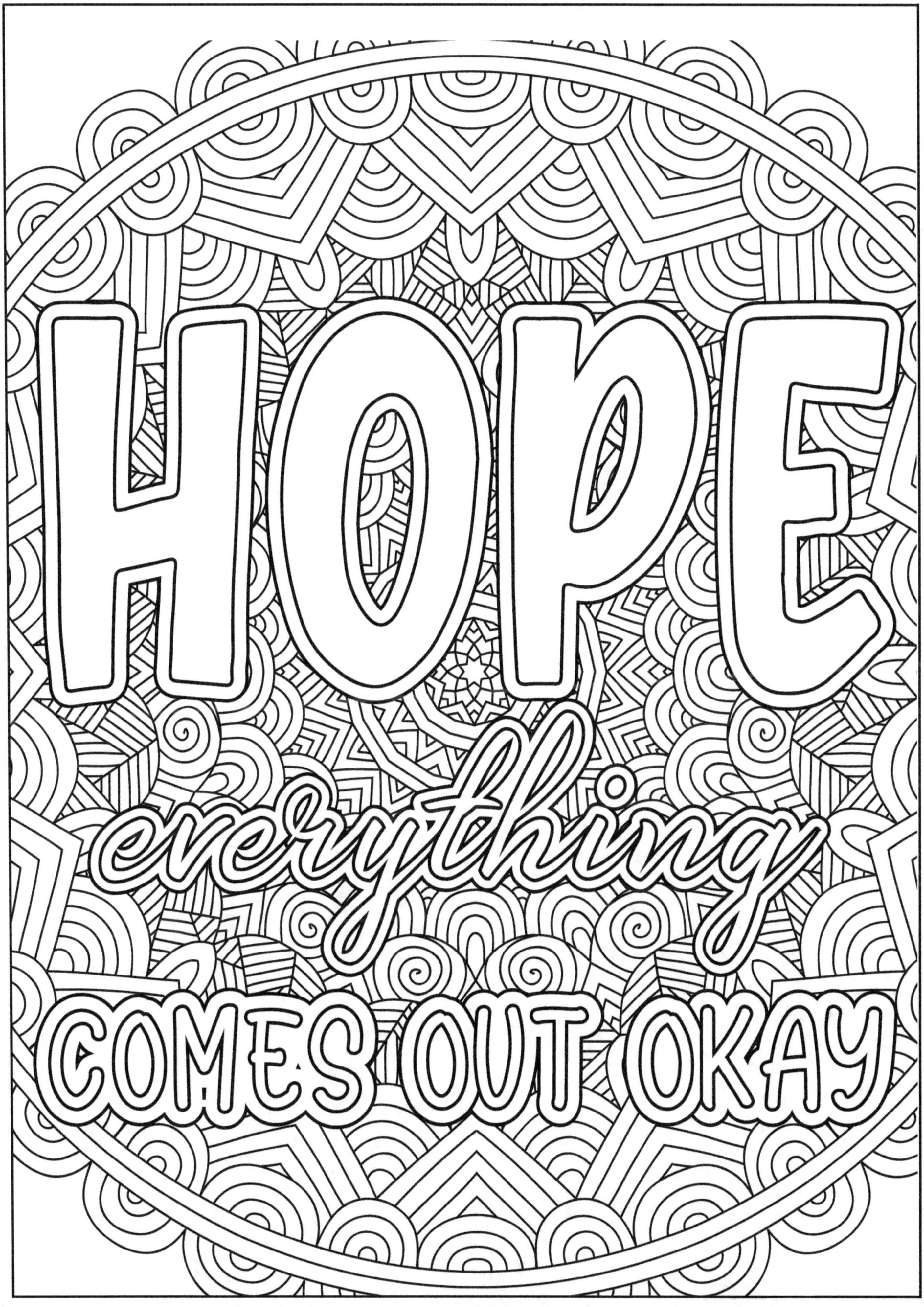
HOPE
everything
COMES OUT OKAY

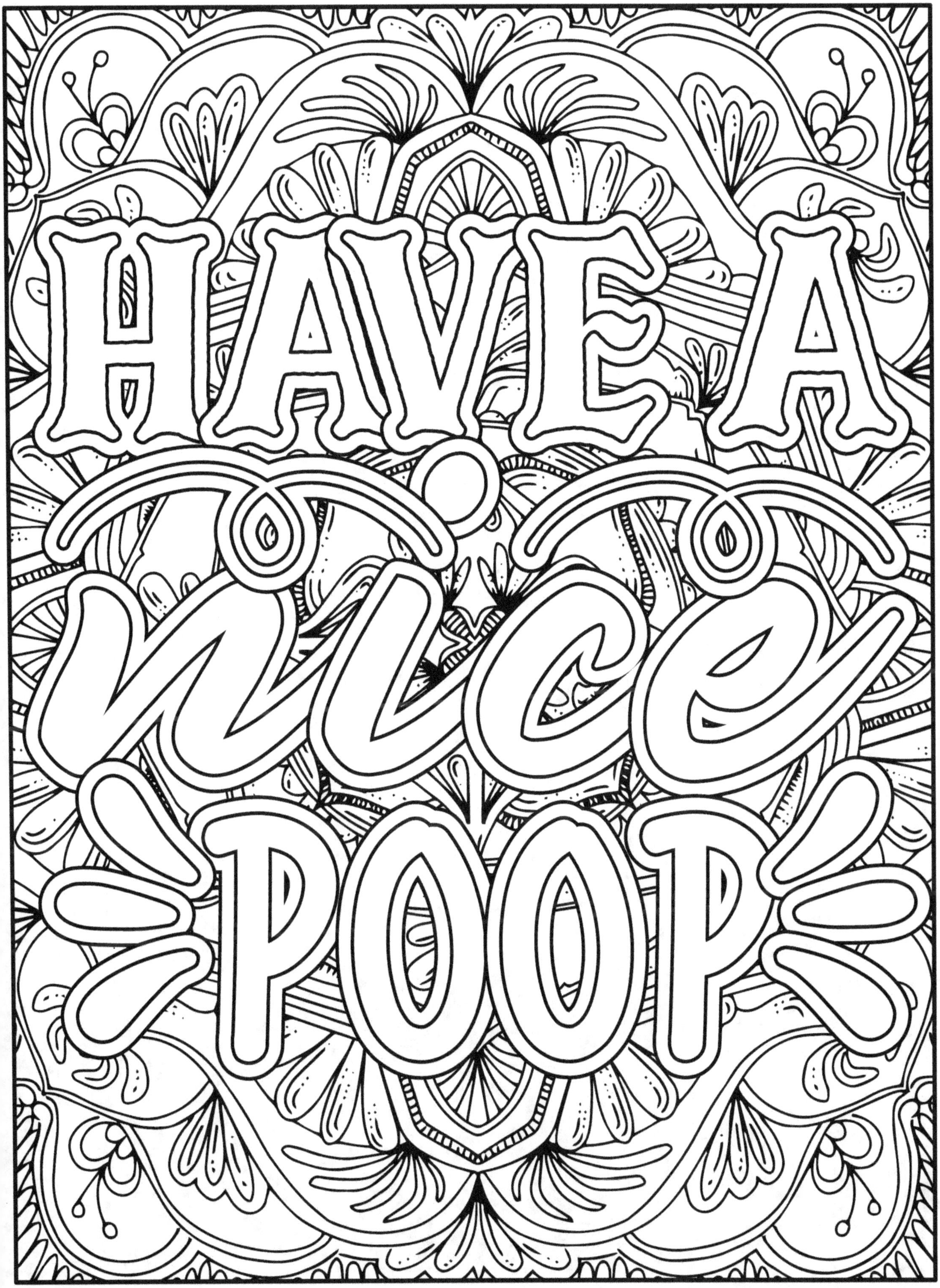
HAVE A
nice
POOP

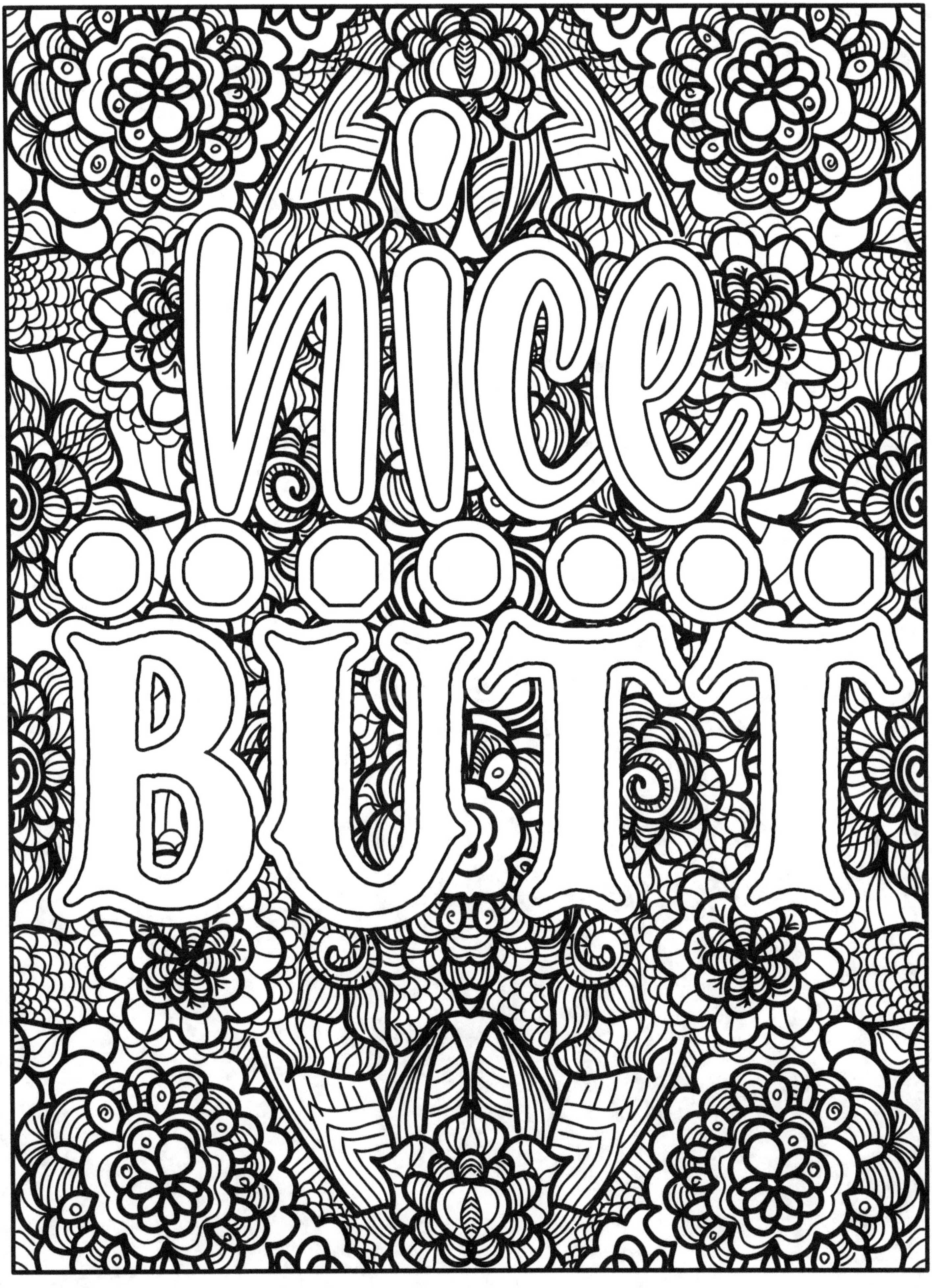
nice
BUTT

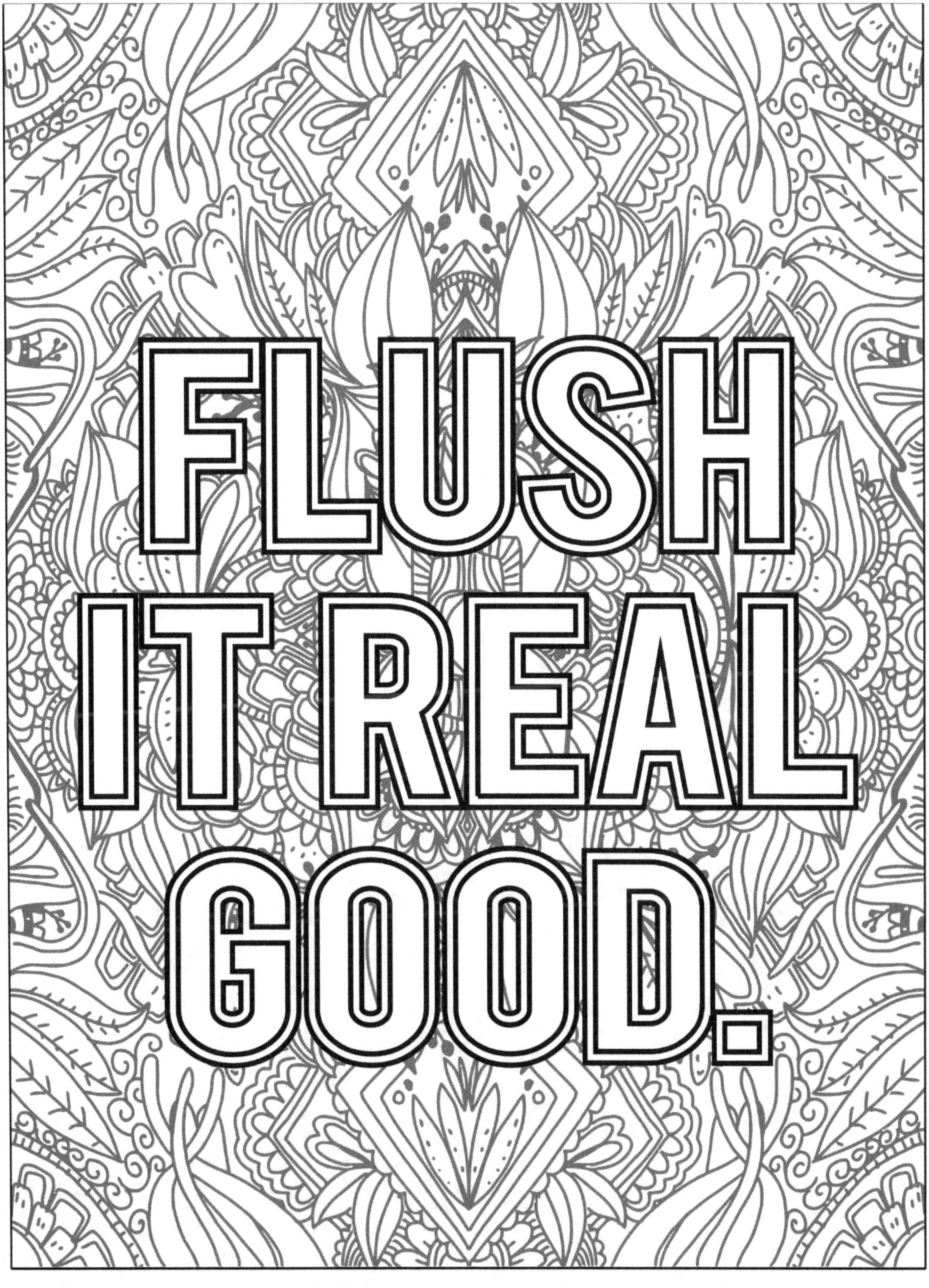
FLUSH
IT REAL
GOOD.

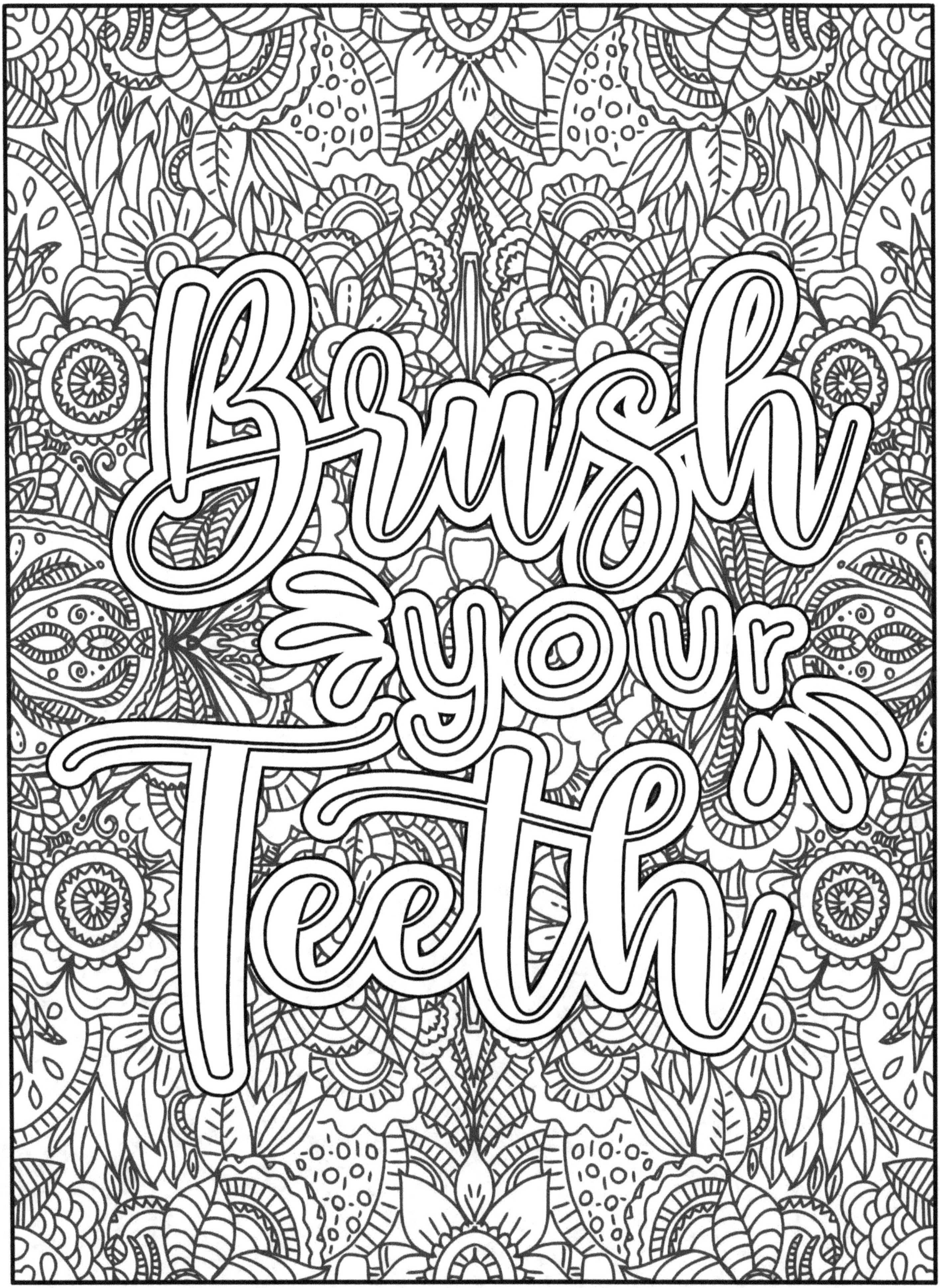
Brush
your
Teeth

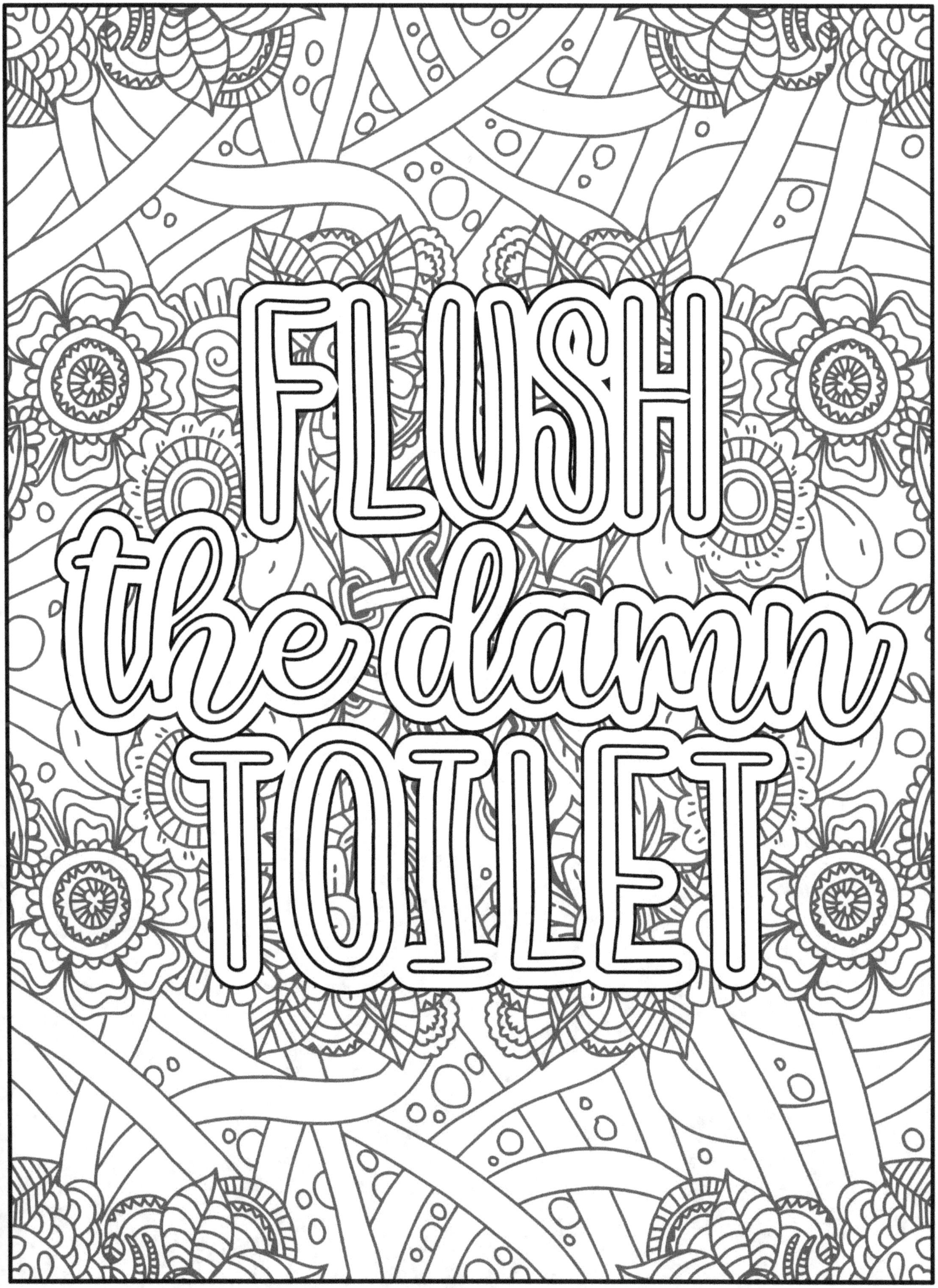
FLUSH
the damn
TOILET

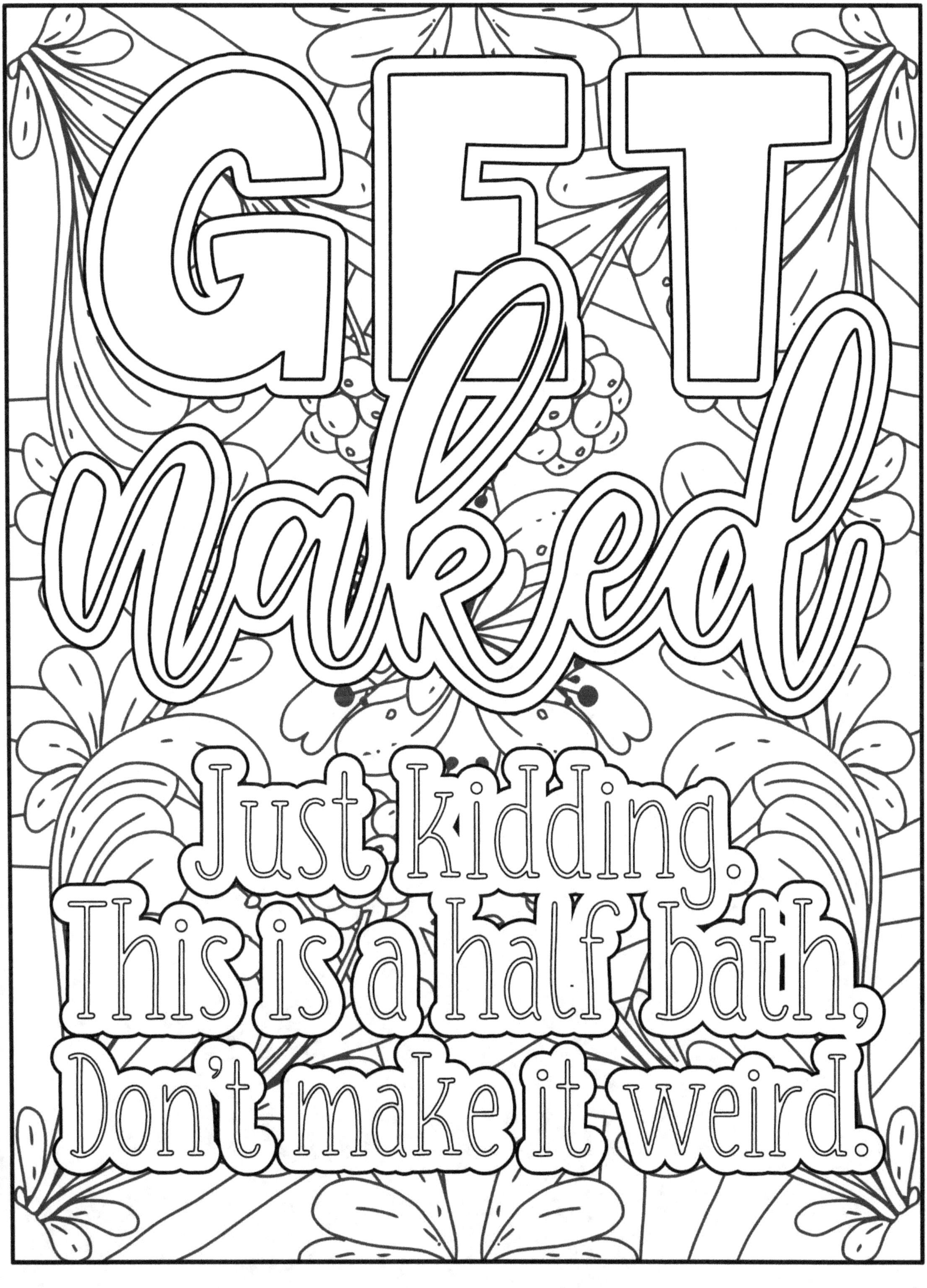
GET
naked
Just kidding.
This is a half bath,
Don't make it weird.

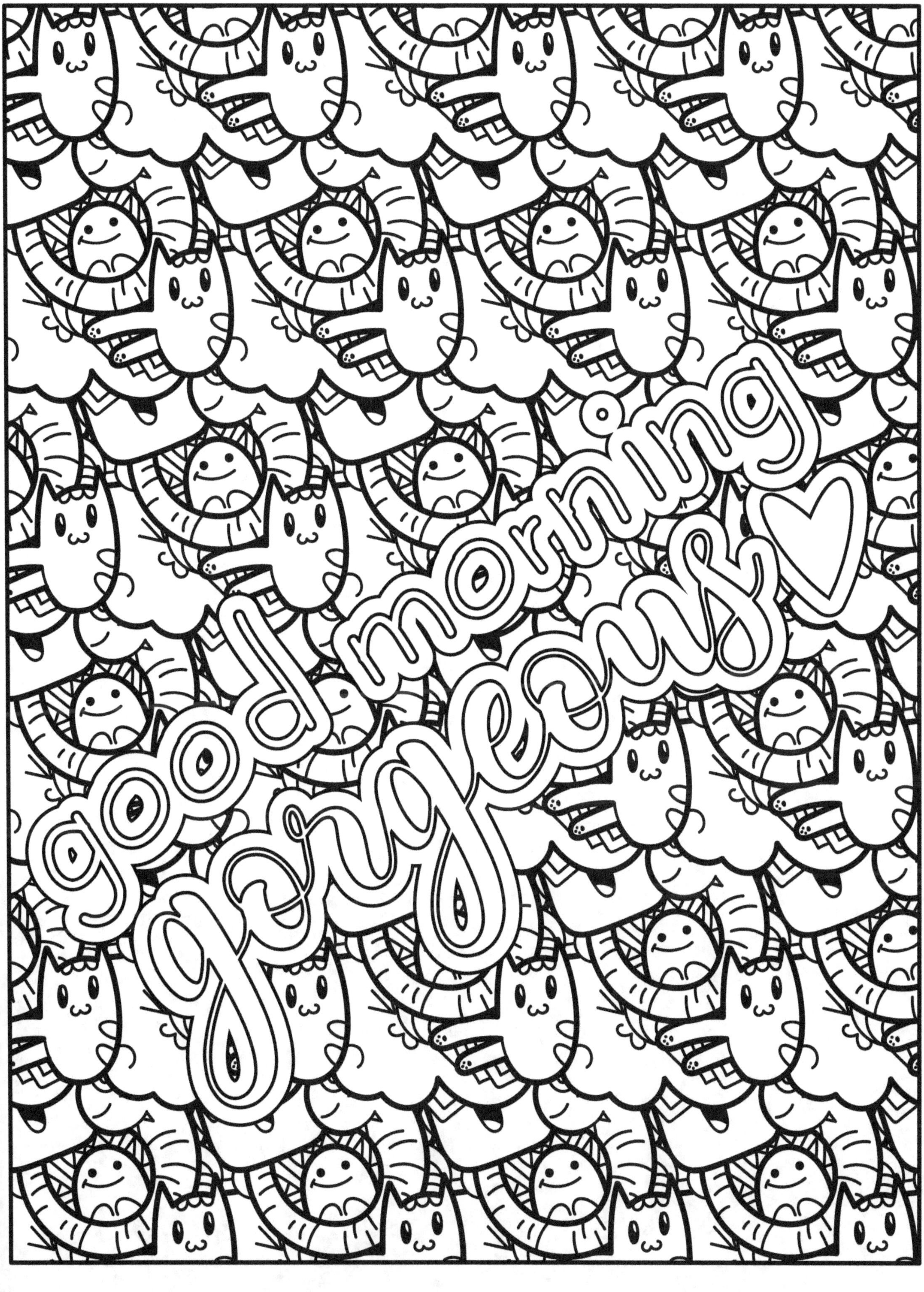
good morning
gorgeous

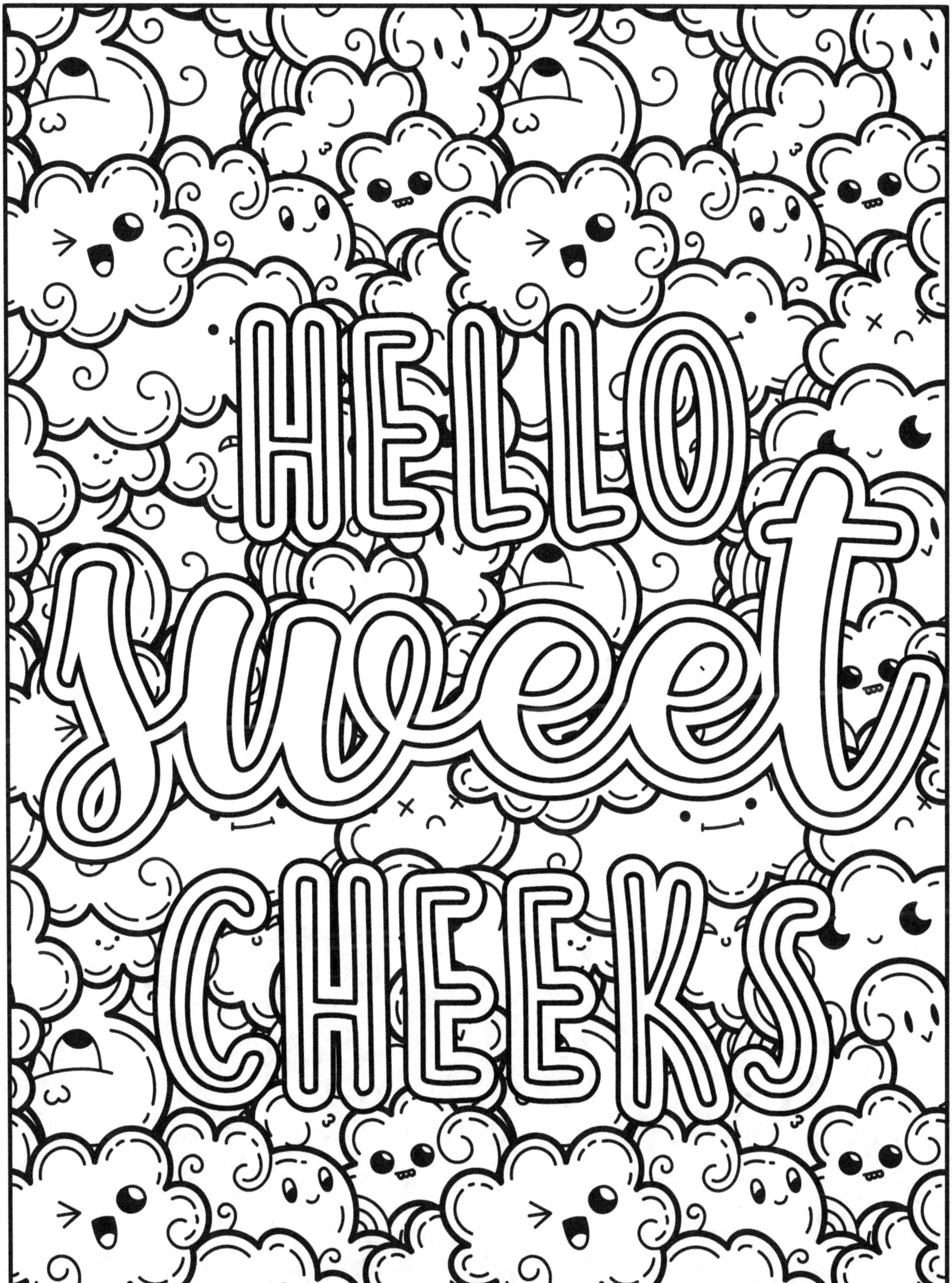
HELLO
sweet
CHEEKS

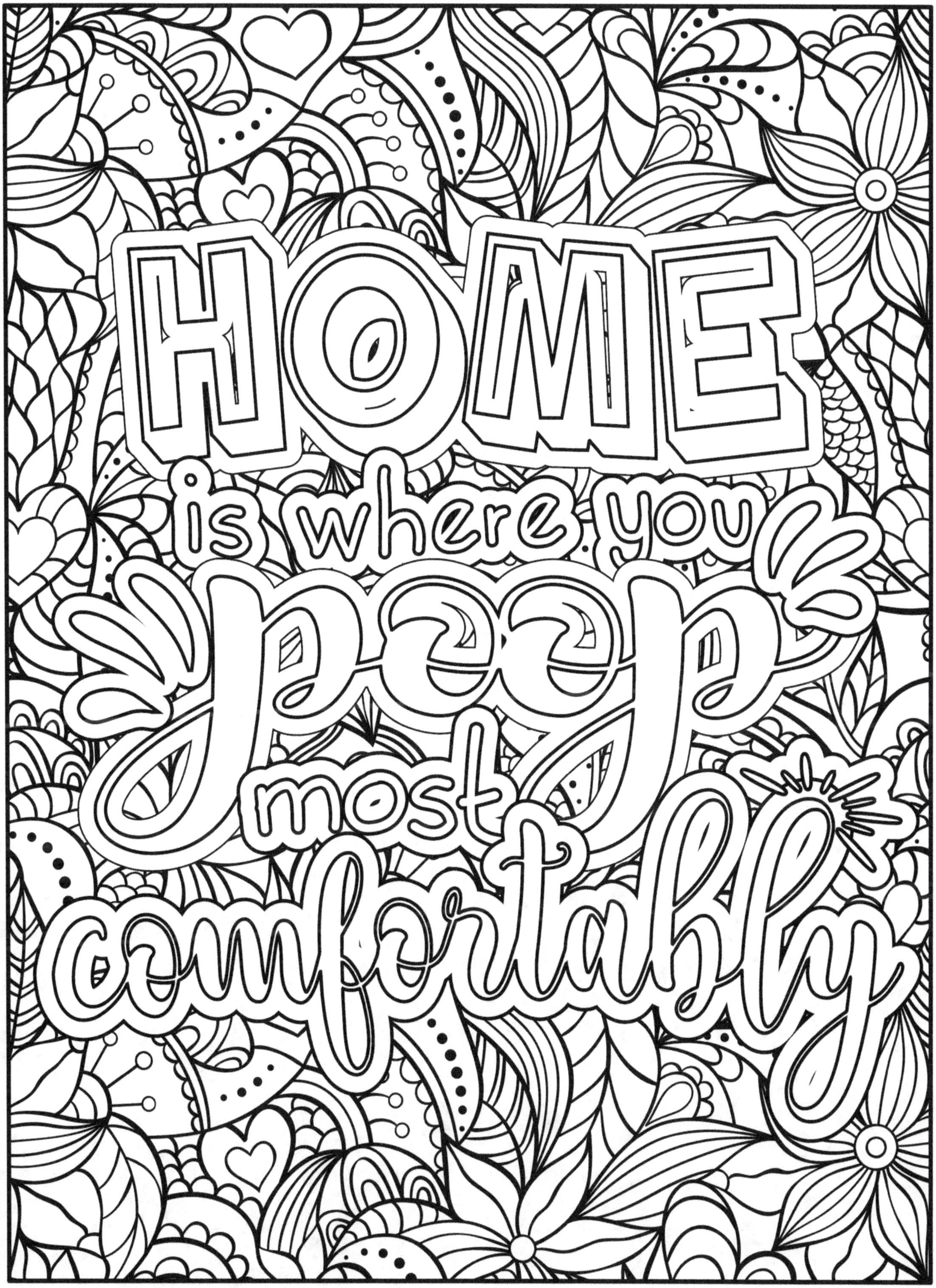
HOME
is where you
poop
most
comfortably

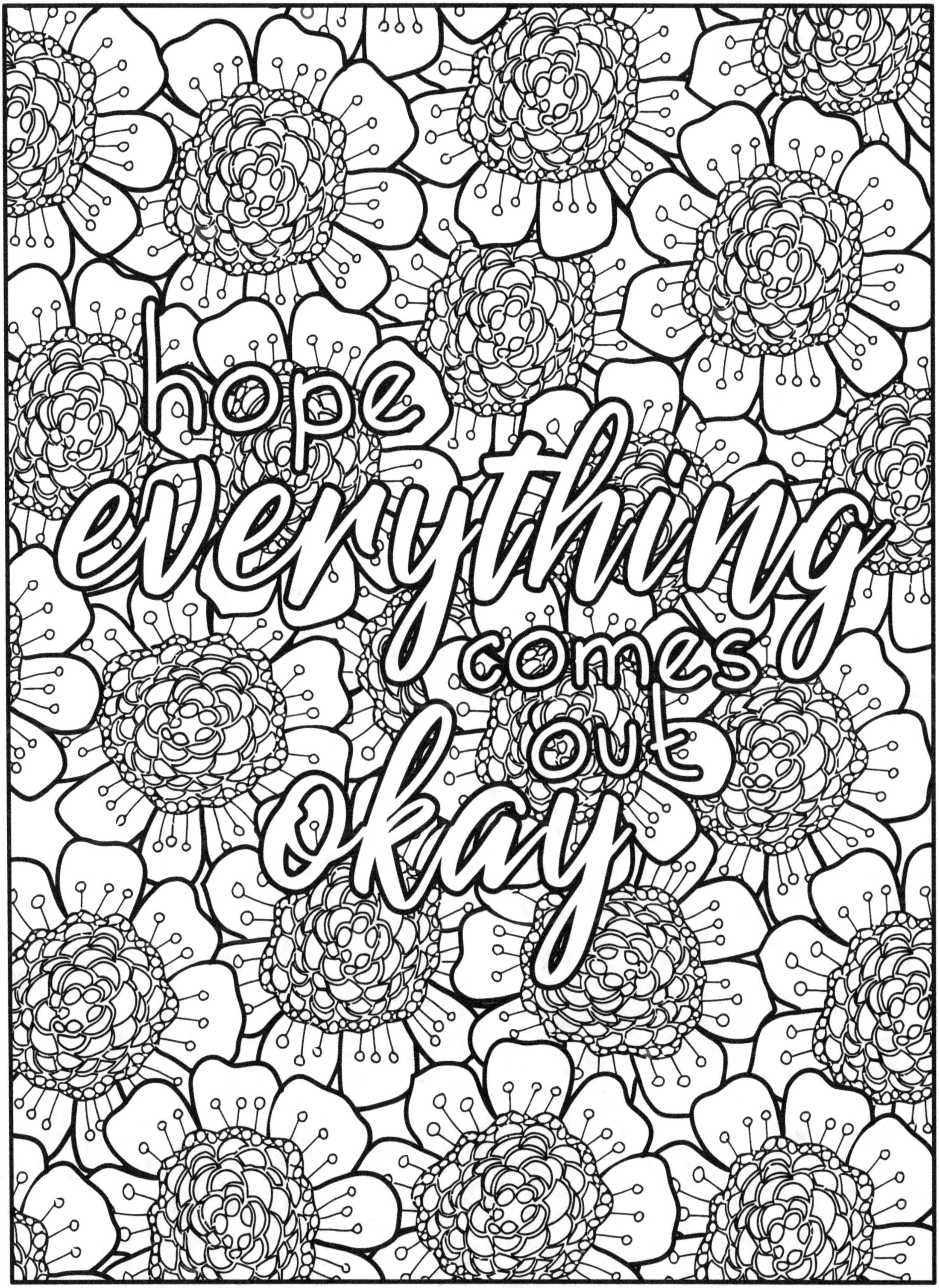
hope
everything
comes
out
okay

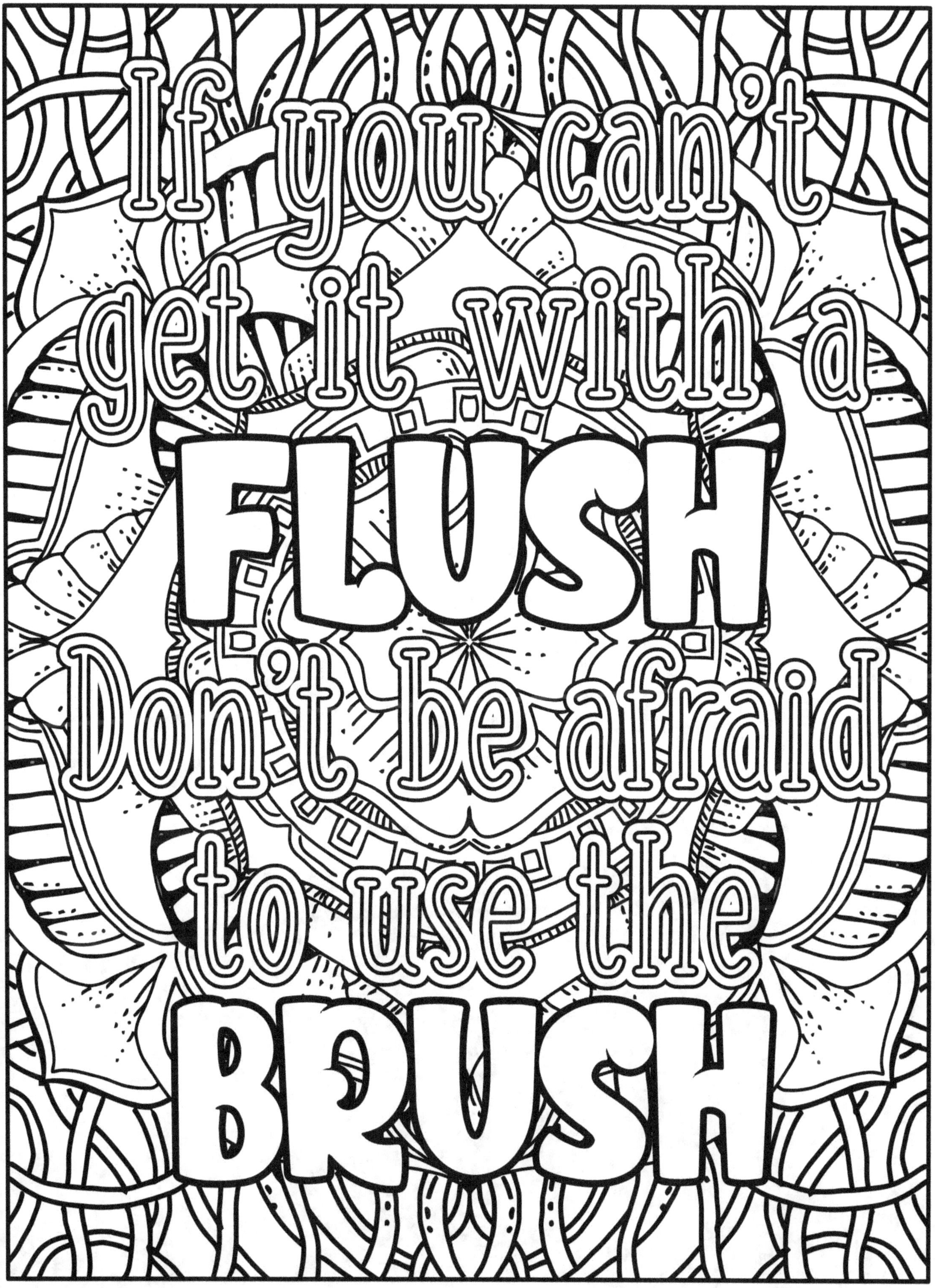
If you can't
get it with a
FLUSH
Don't be afraid
to use the
BRUSH

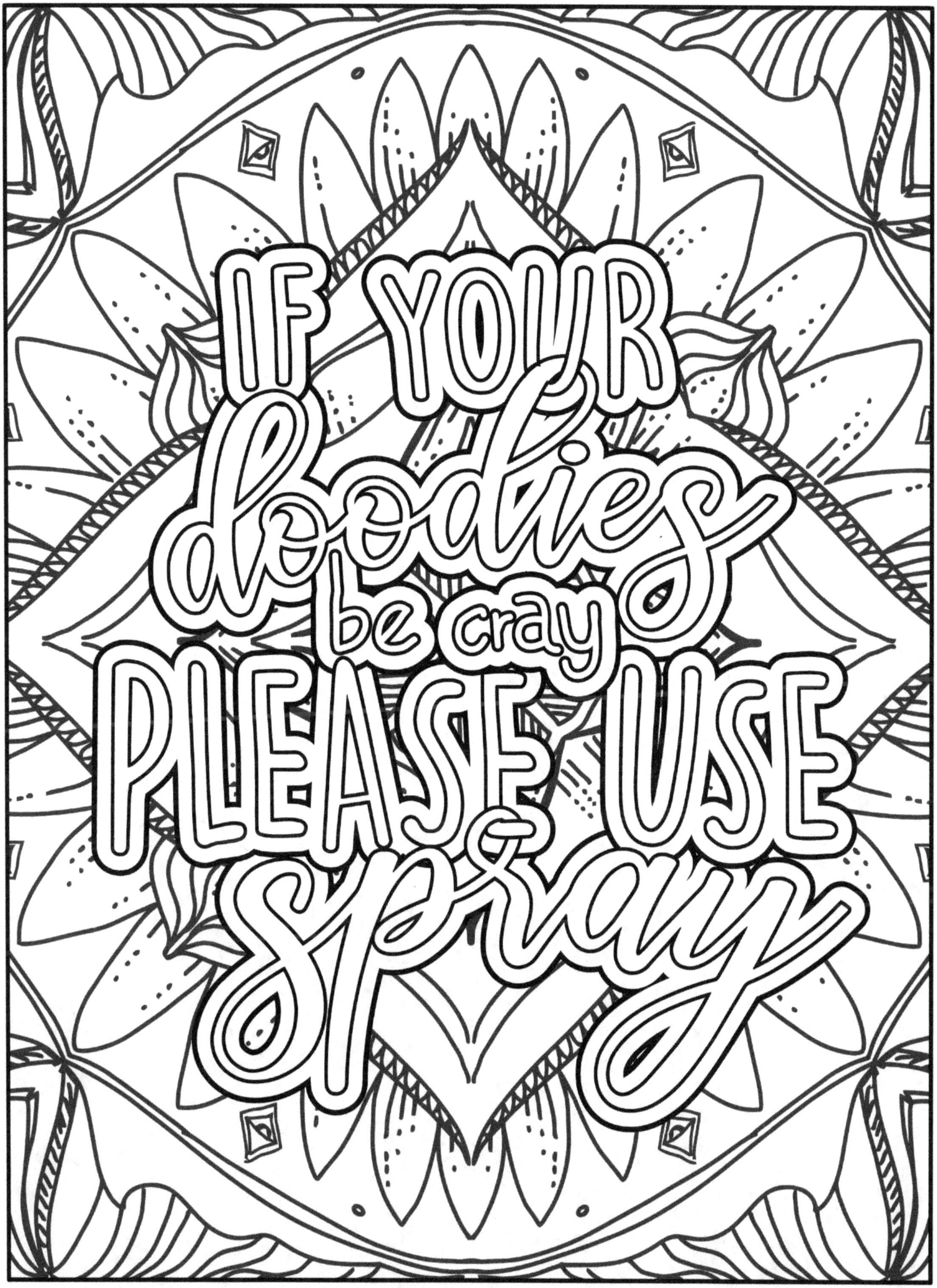
IF YOUR
doodies
be cray
PLEASE USE
&
Spray

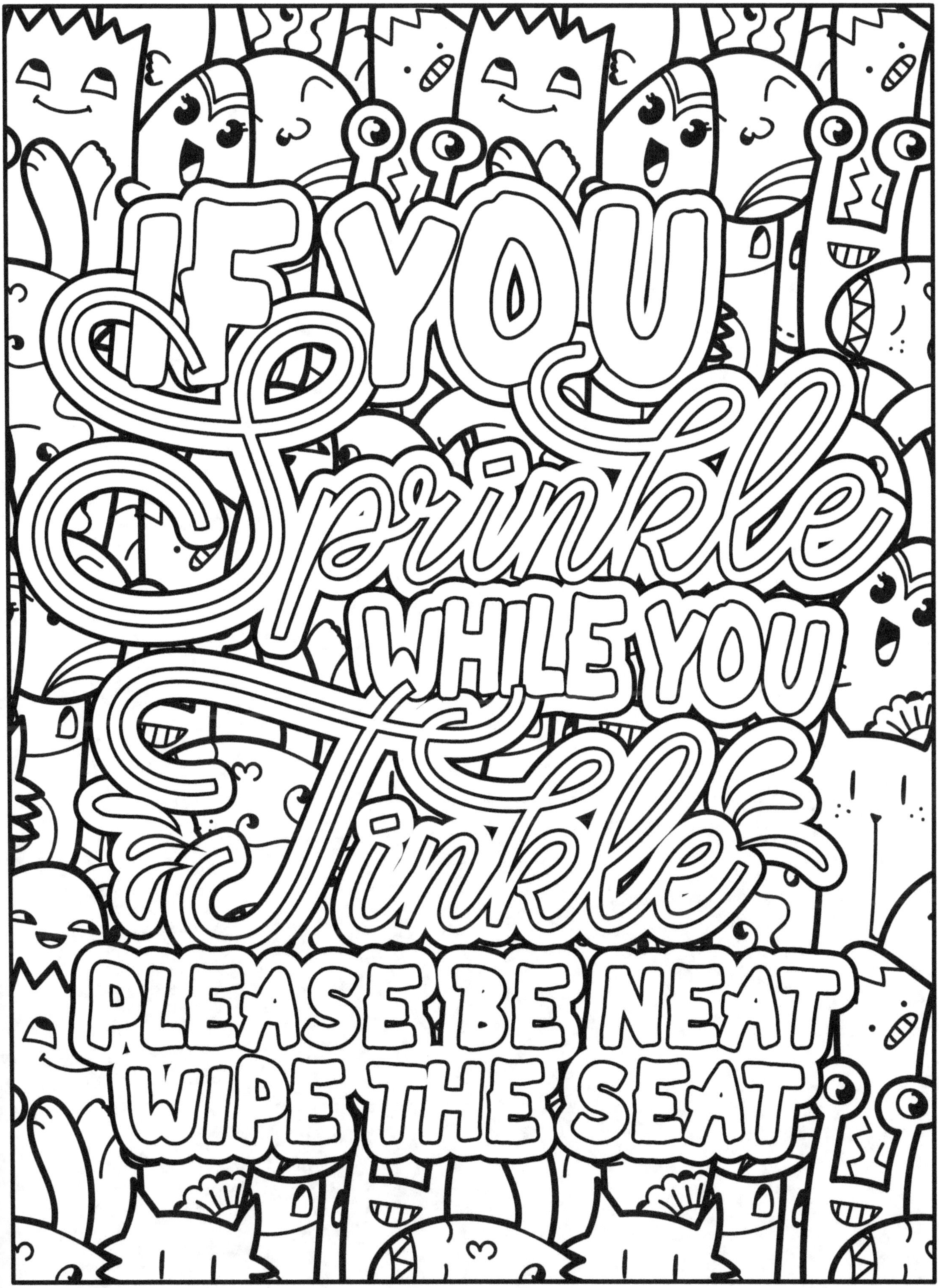
IF YOU
Sprinkle
WHILE YOU
Tinkle
PLEASE BE NEAT
WIPE THE SEAT

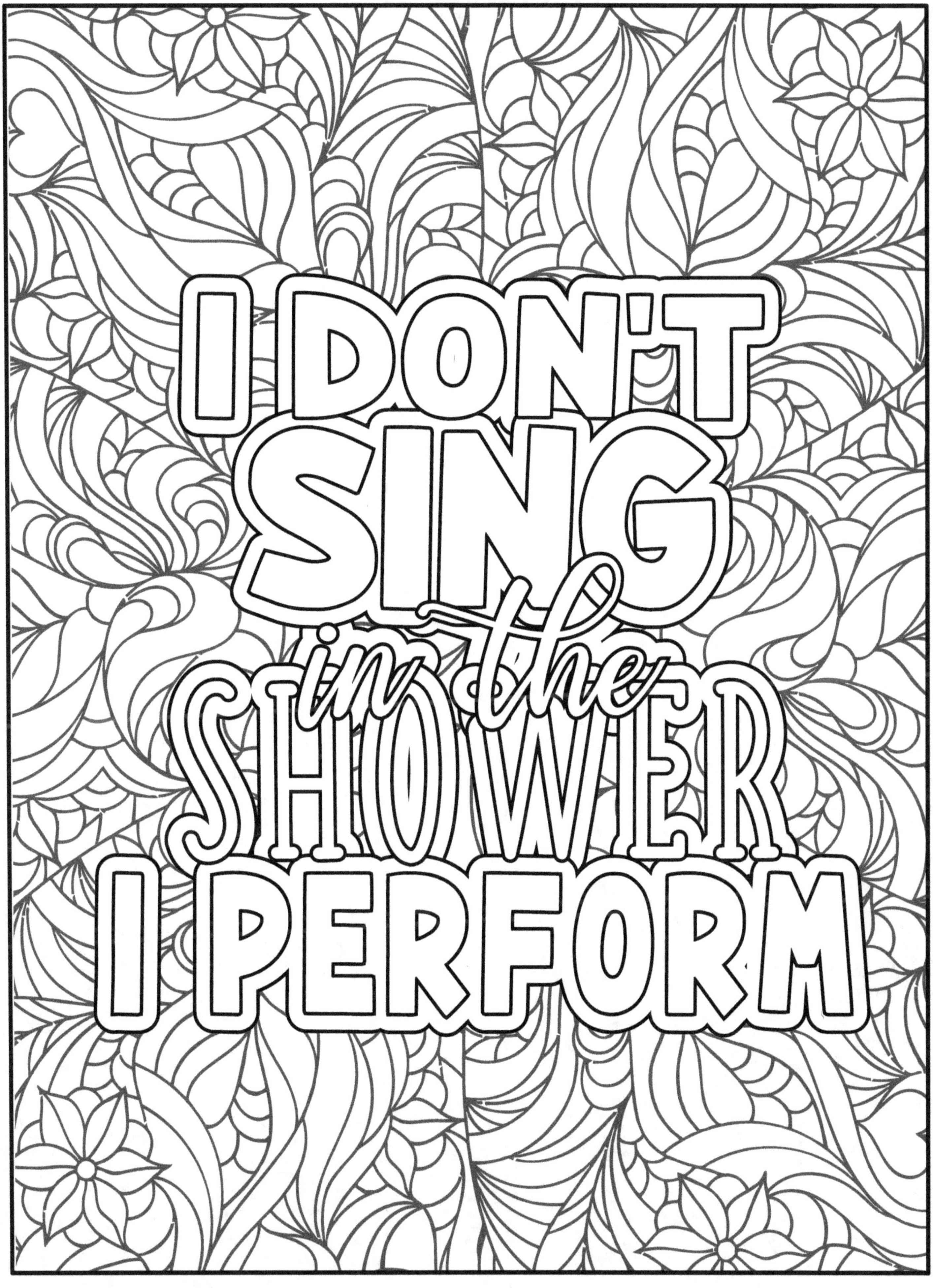
I DON'T
SING
in the
SHOWER
I PERFORM

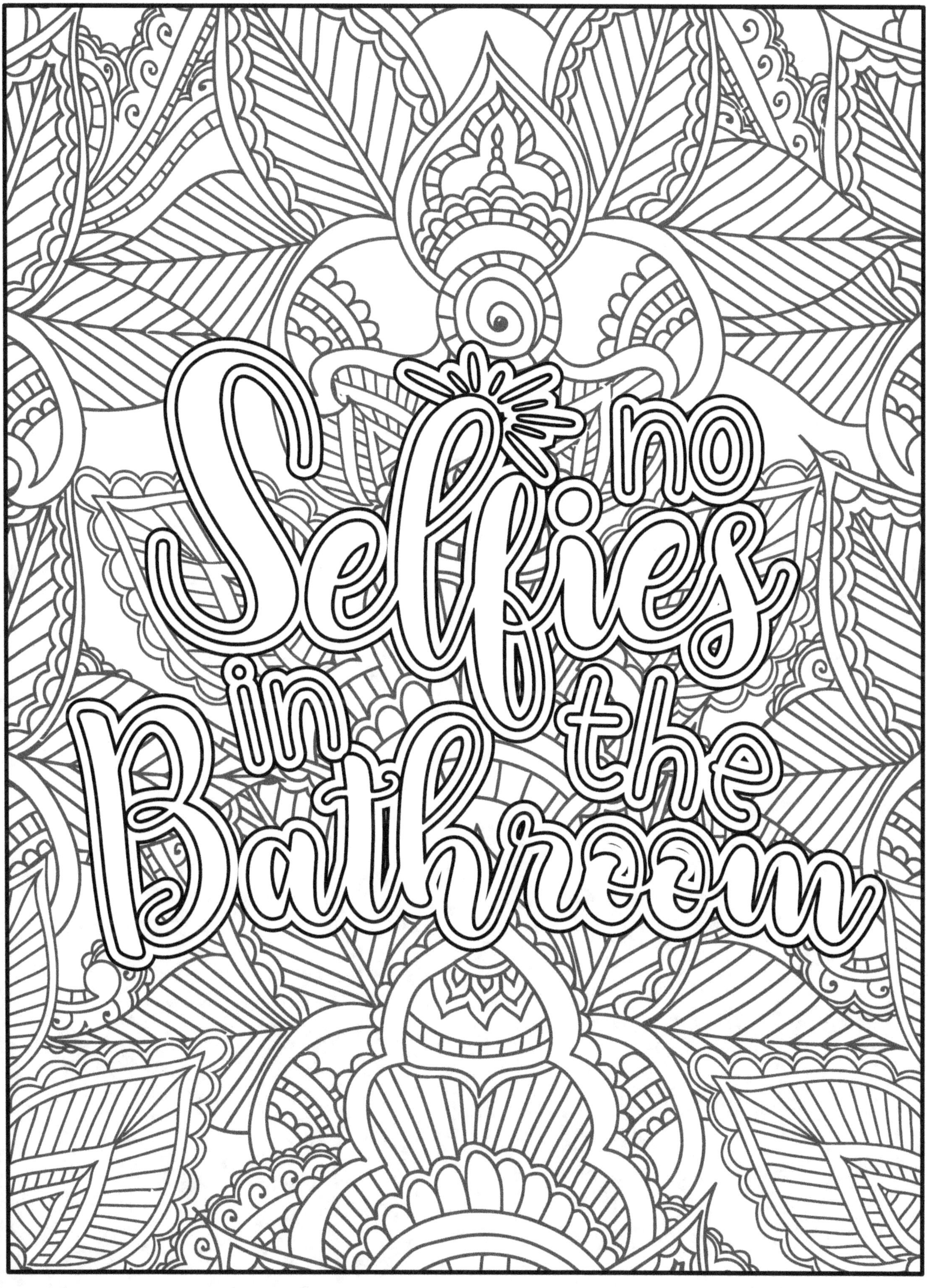
no Selfies in the Bathroom

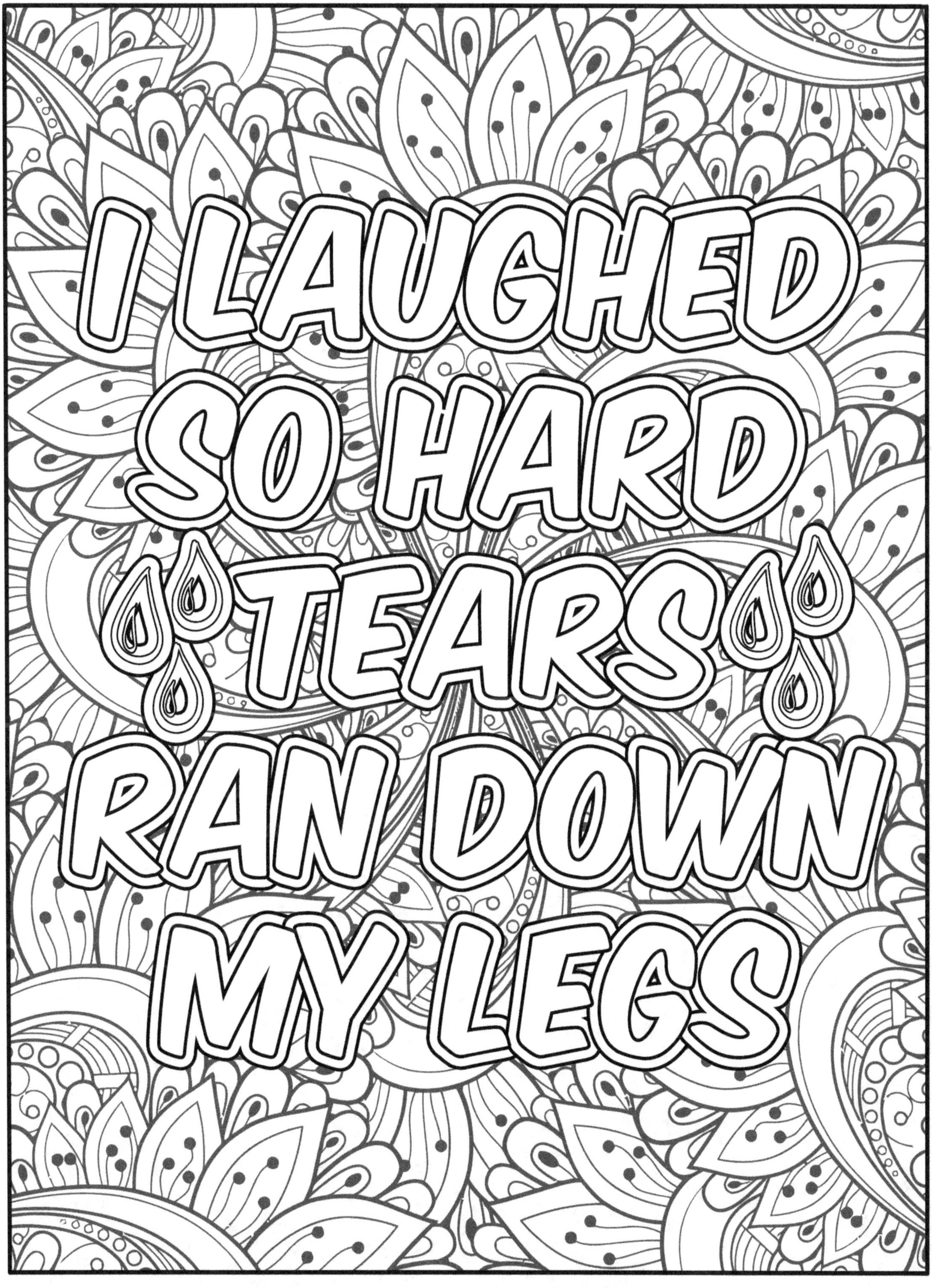
I LAUGHED
SO HARD
TEARS
RAN DOWN
MY LEGS

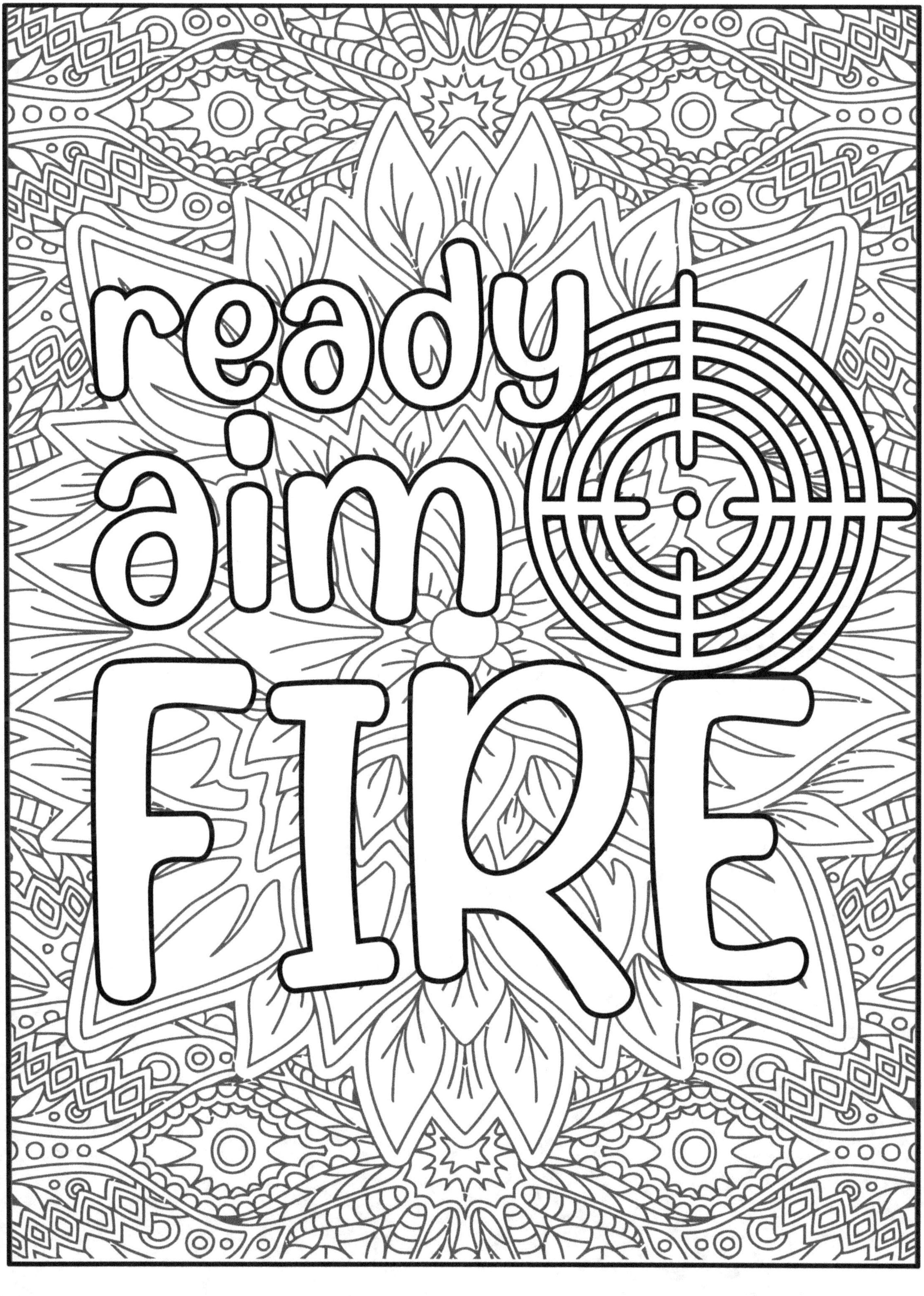
ready
aim
FIRE

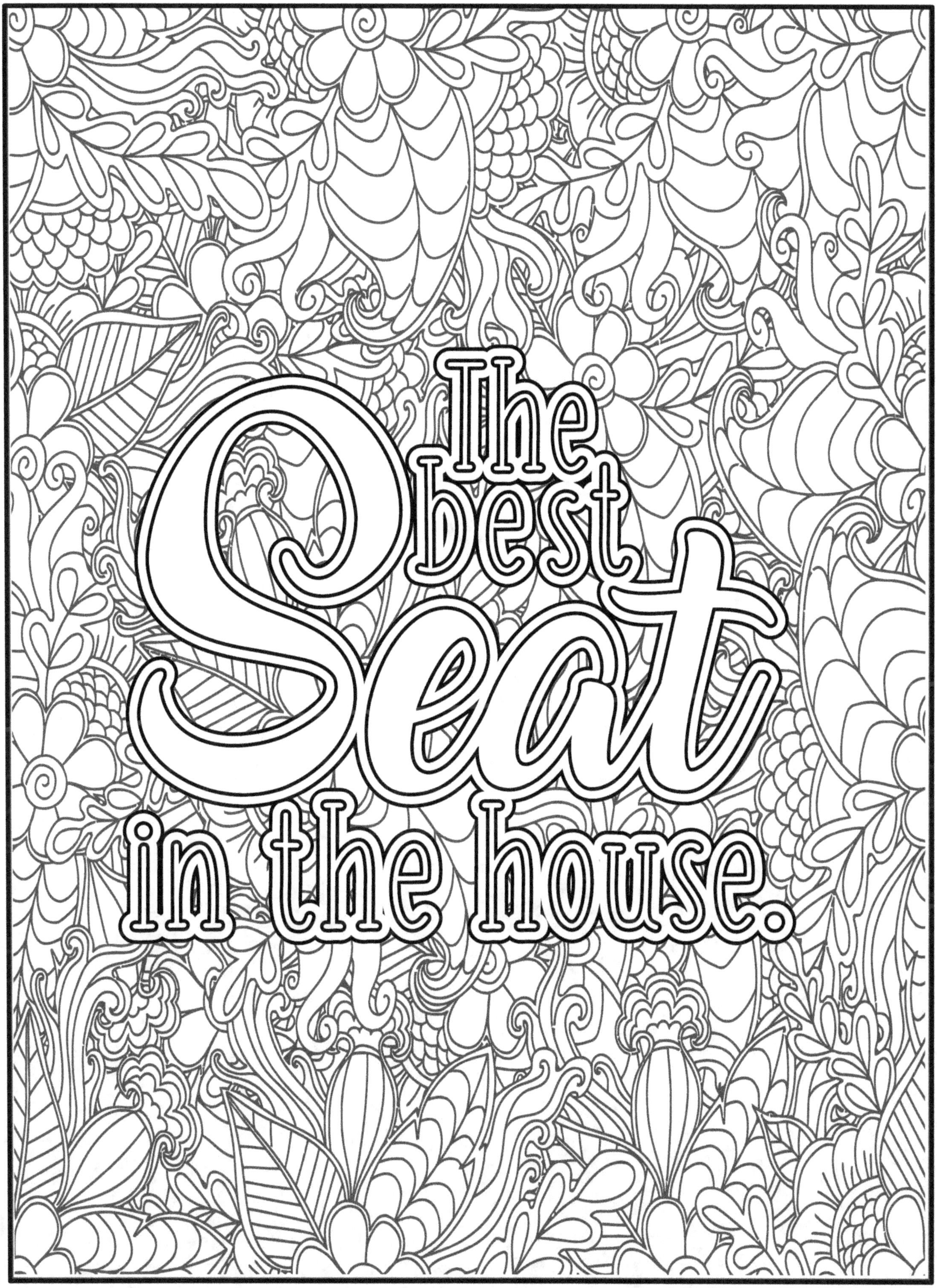
The best Seat in the house.

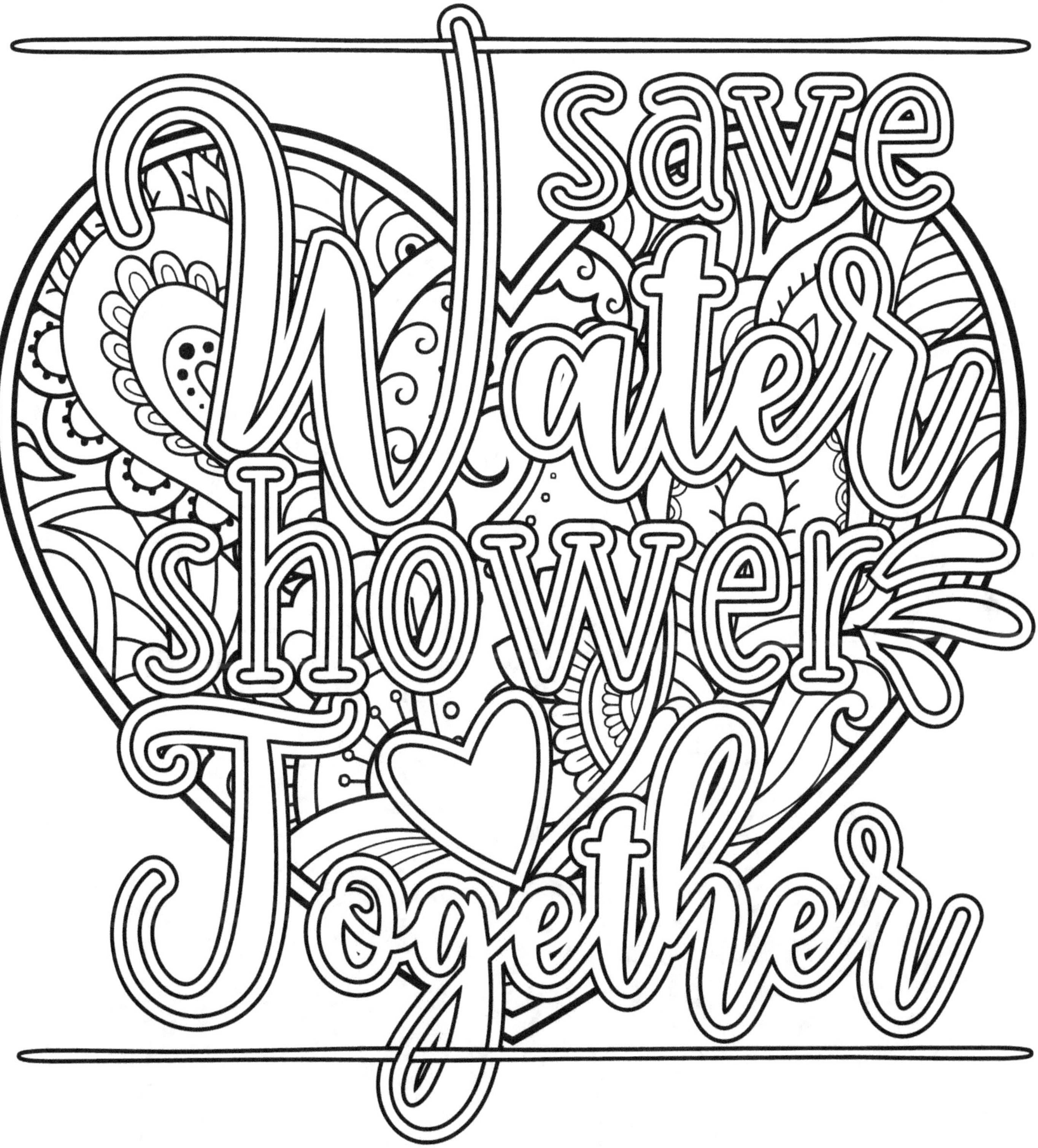
I save
Water
shower
Together

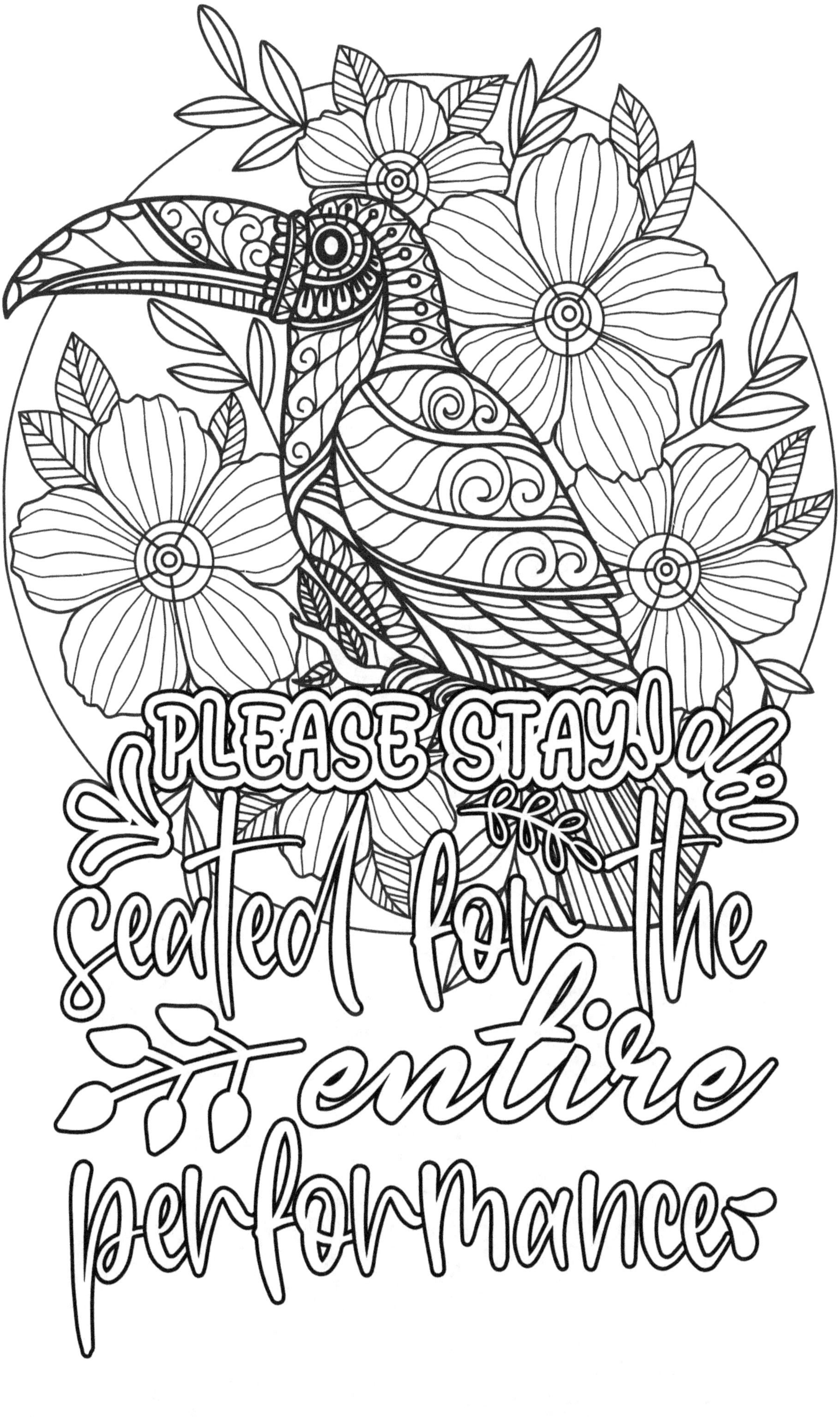
PLEASE STAY
seated for the
entire
performance

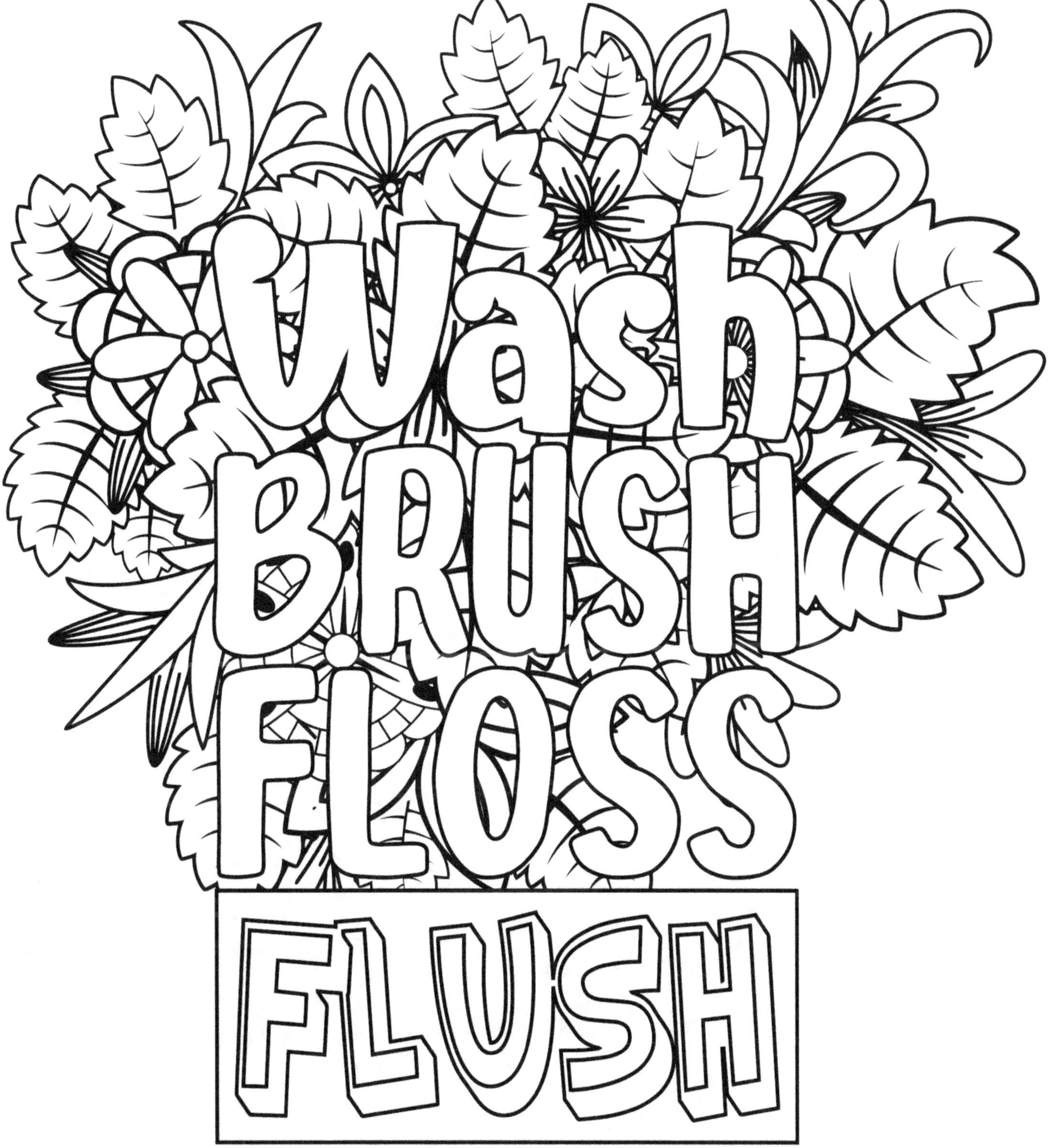
Wash
BRUSH
FLOSS
FLUSH

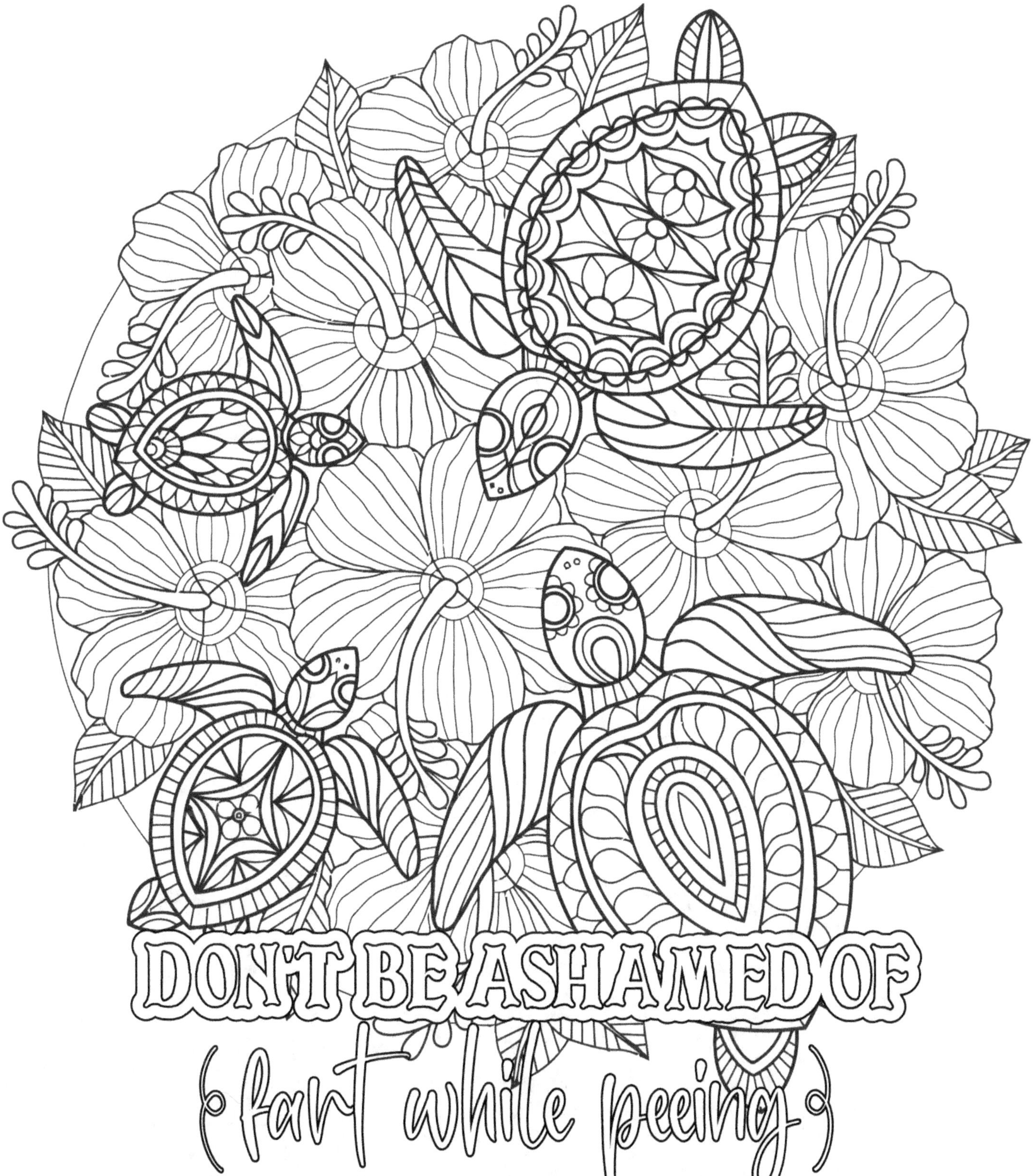

DON'T BE ASHAMED OF

(fart while peeing)

REMEMBER RAIN SOMETIMES

comes with thunder

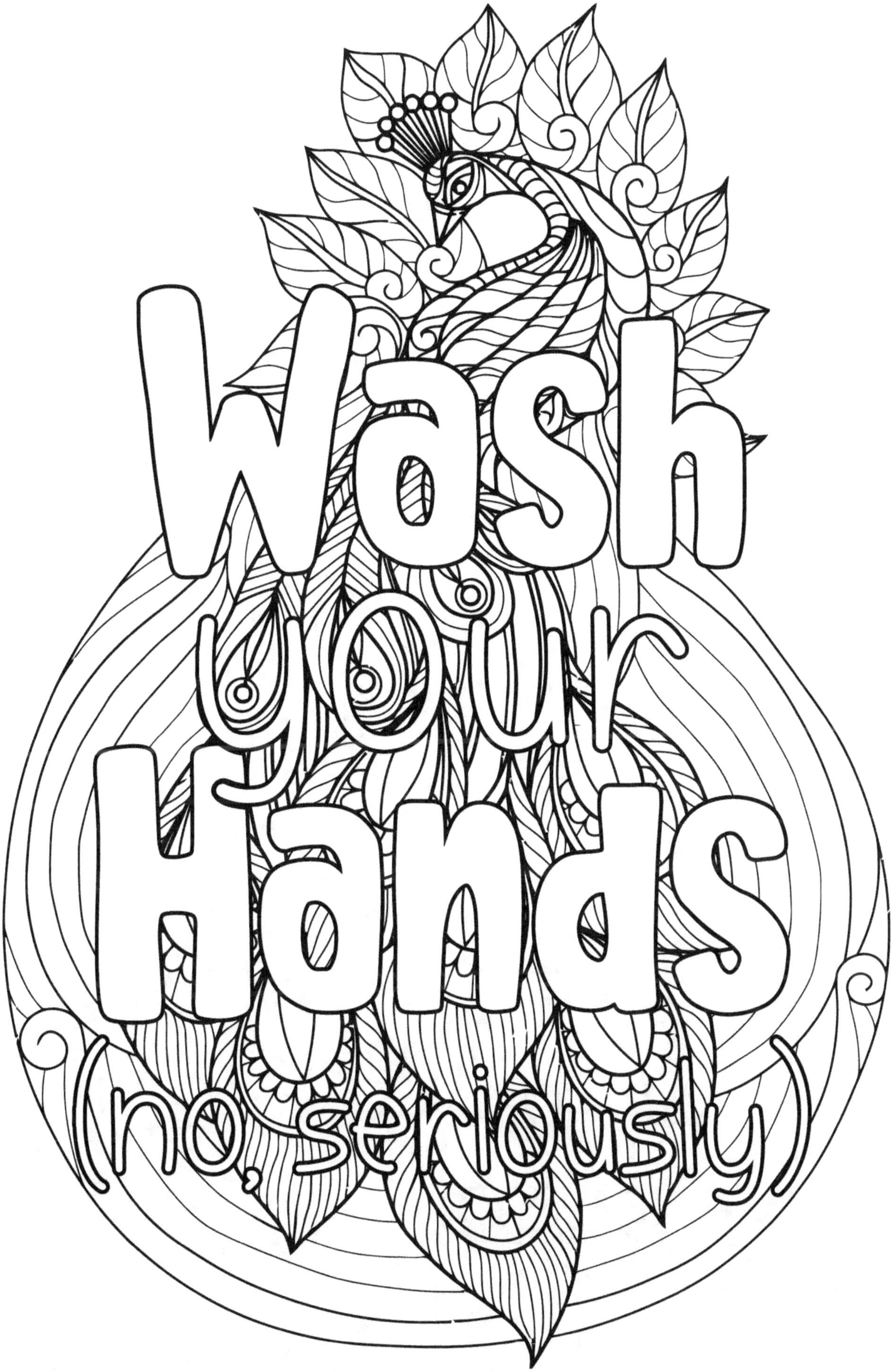
Wash
your
Hands
(no, seriously)

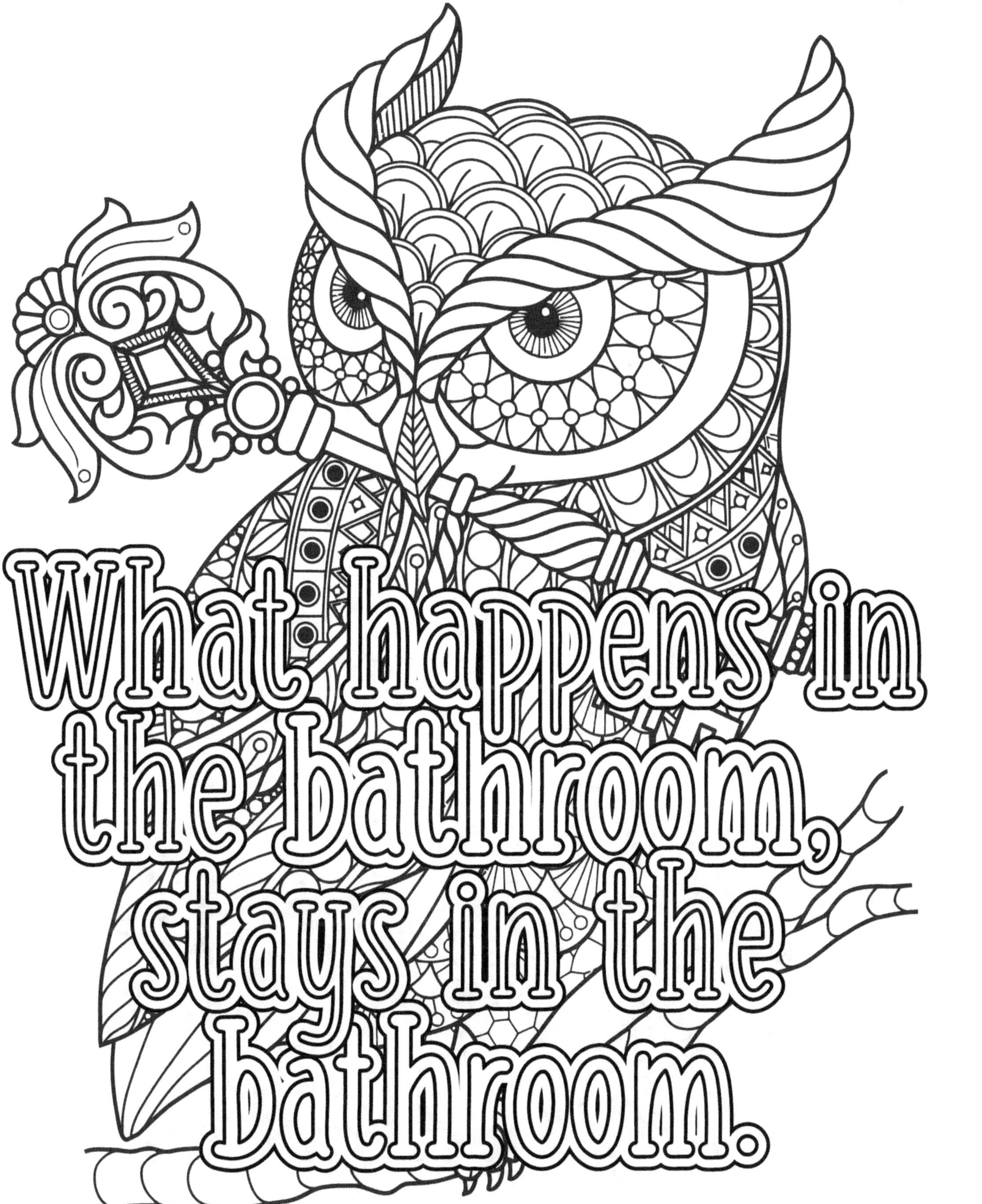
What happens in
the bathroom,
stays in the
bathroom.

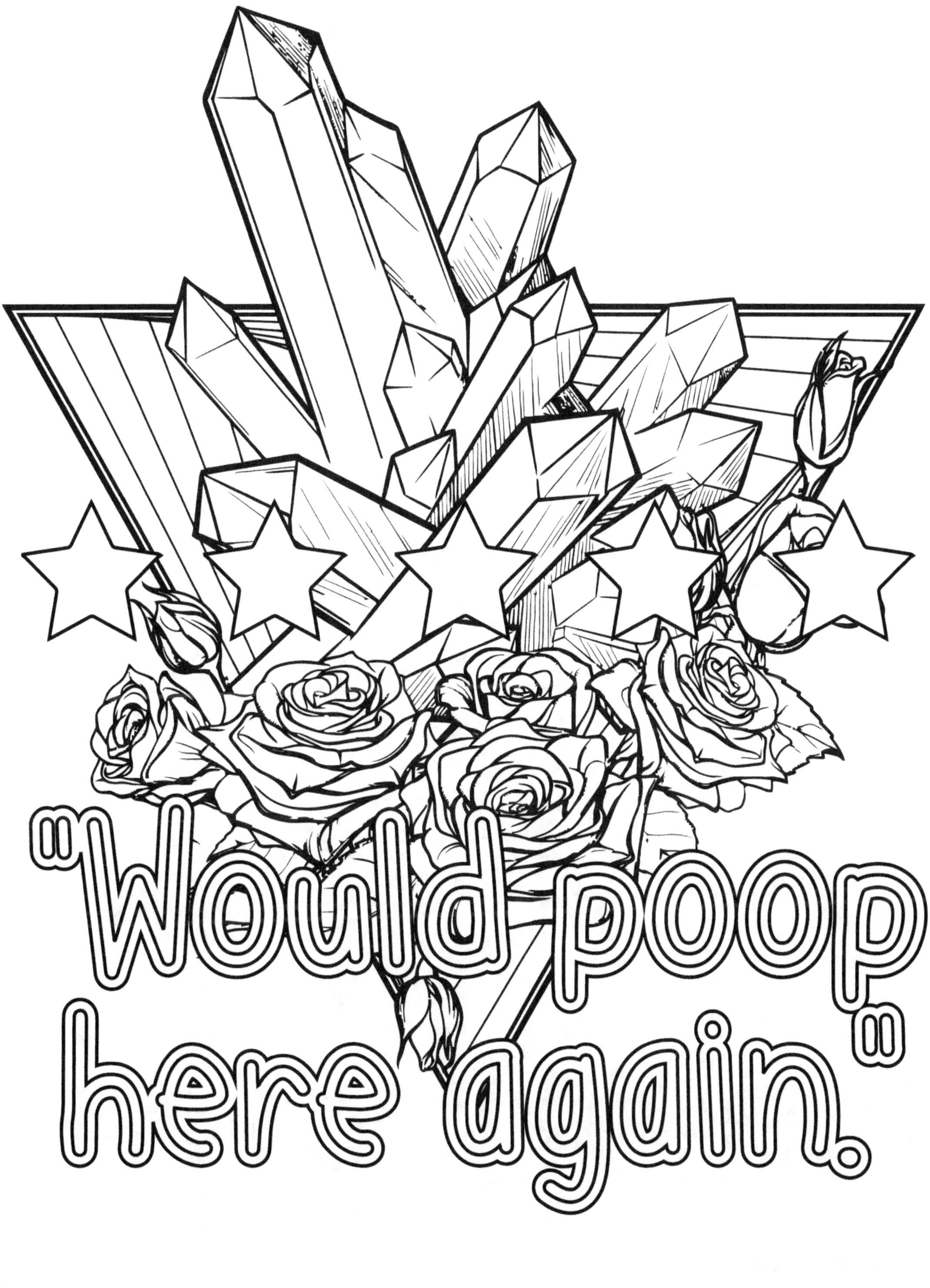
"Would poop here again."

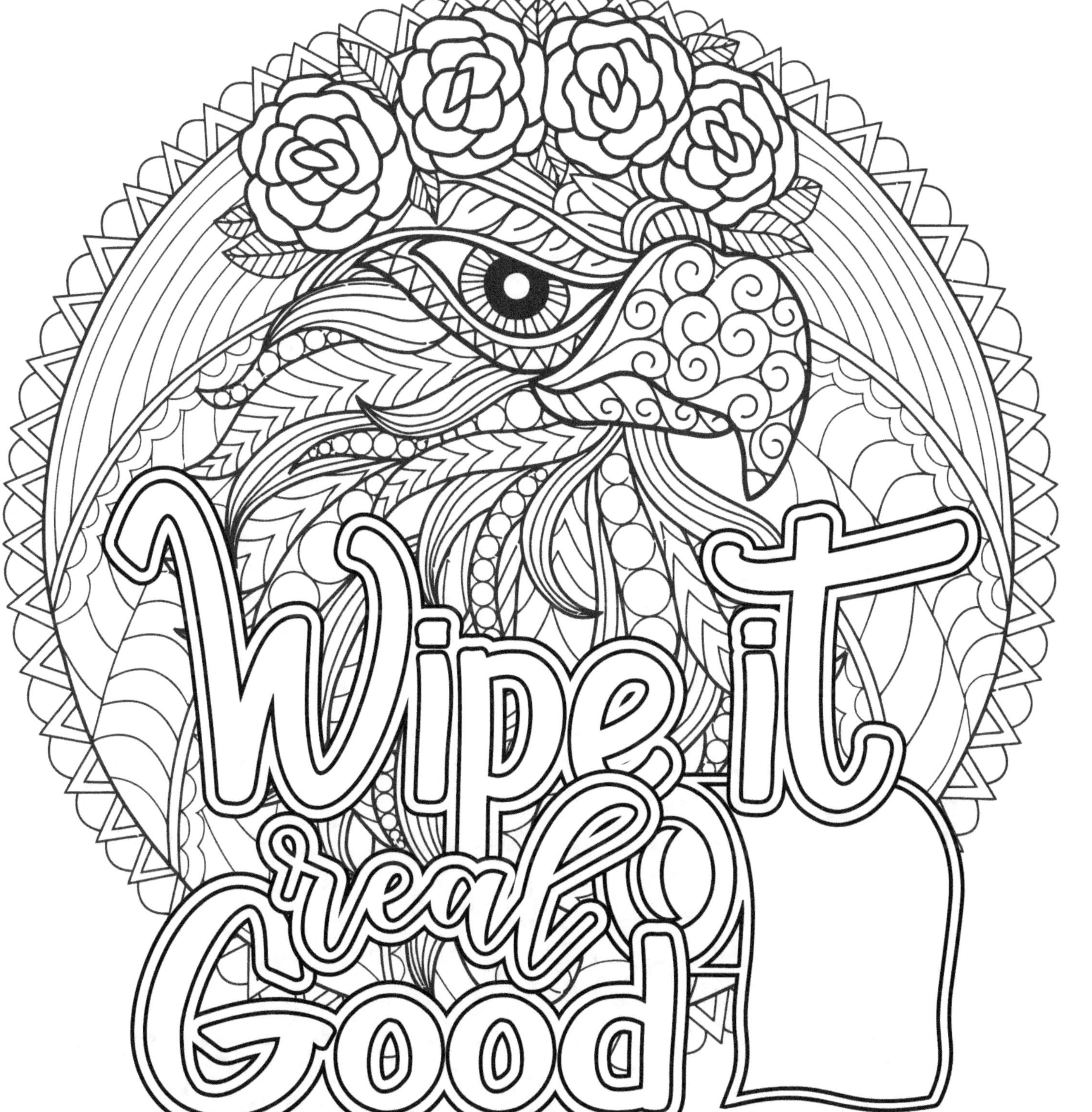
Wipe it
real
Good

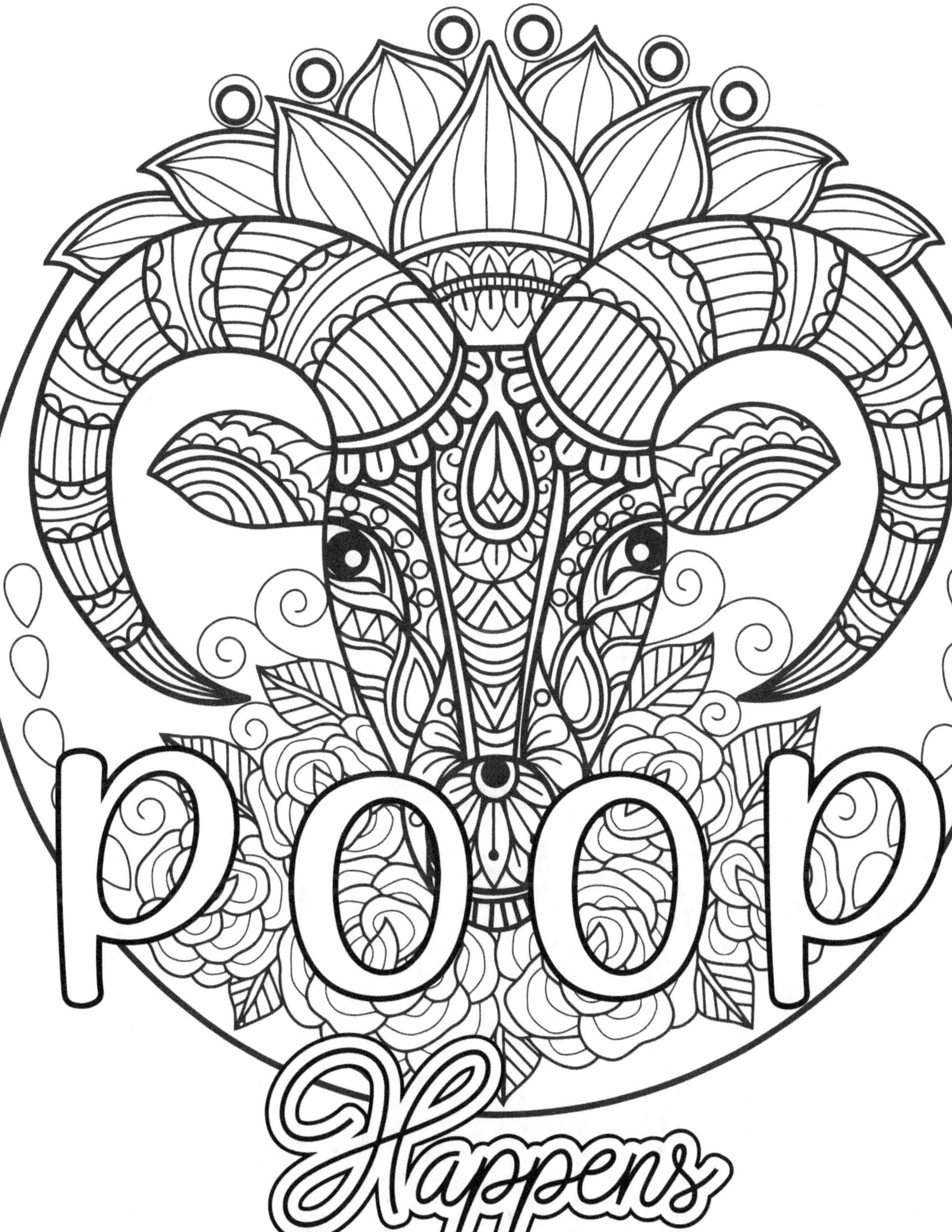
poop
Happens

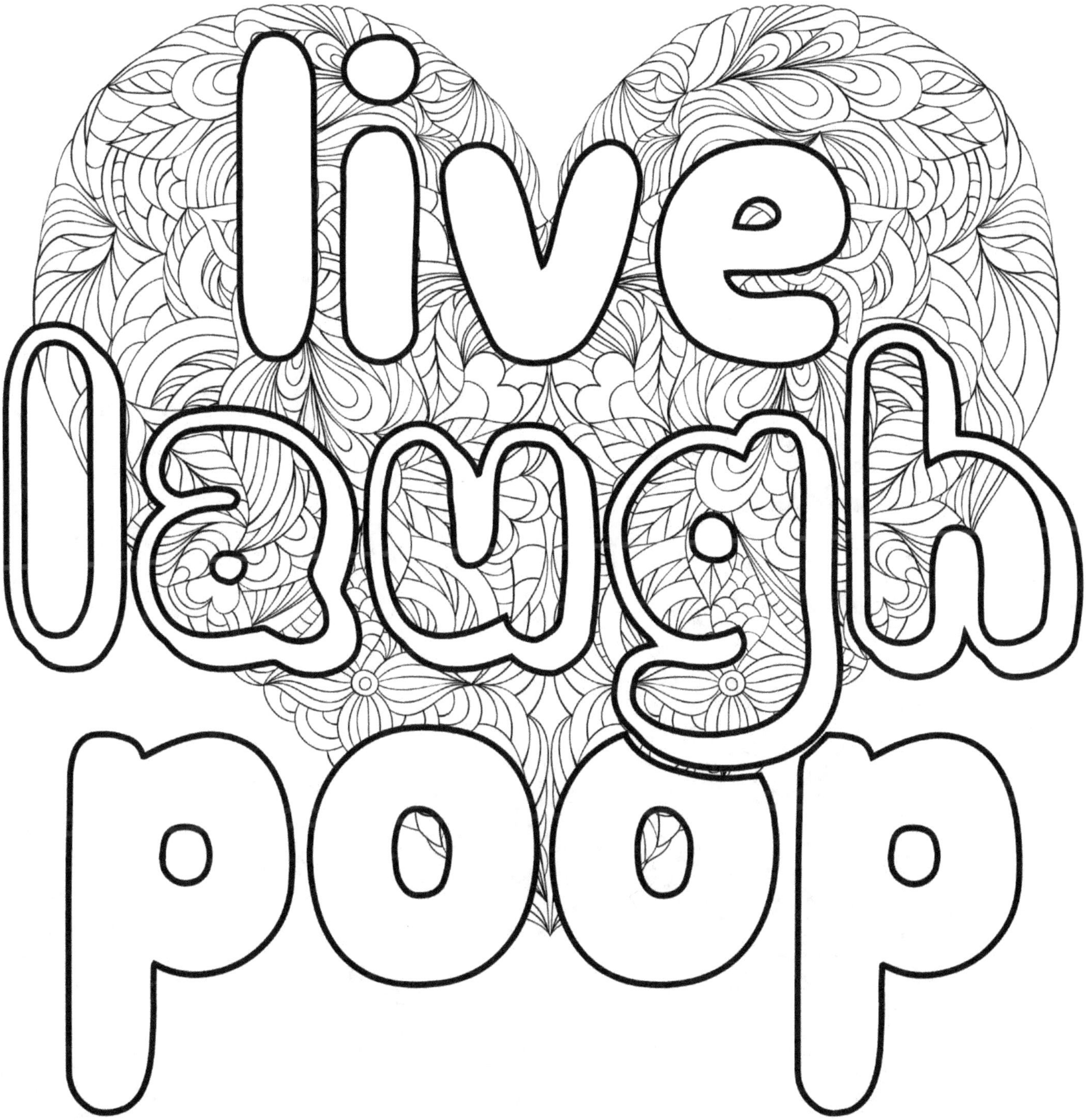
live
laugh
poop

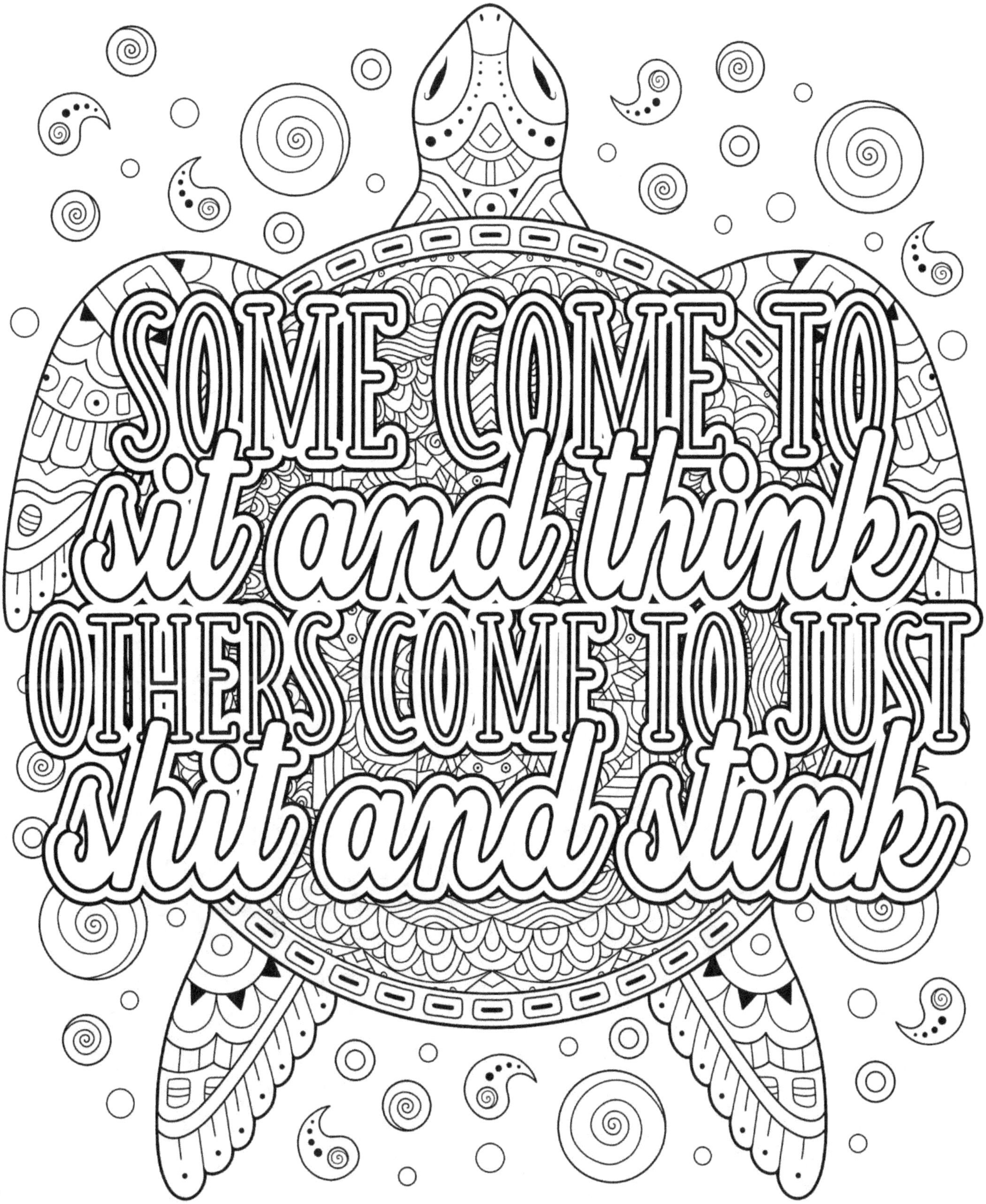
SOME COME TO
sit and think
OTHERS COME TO JUST
shit and stink

HERE I SIT BROKEN

hearted had

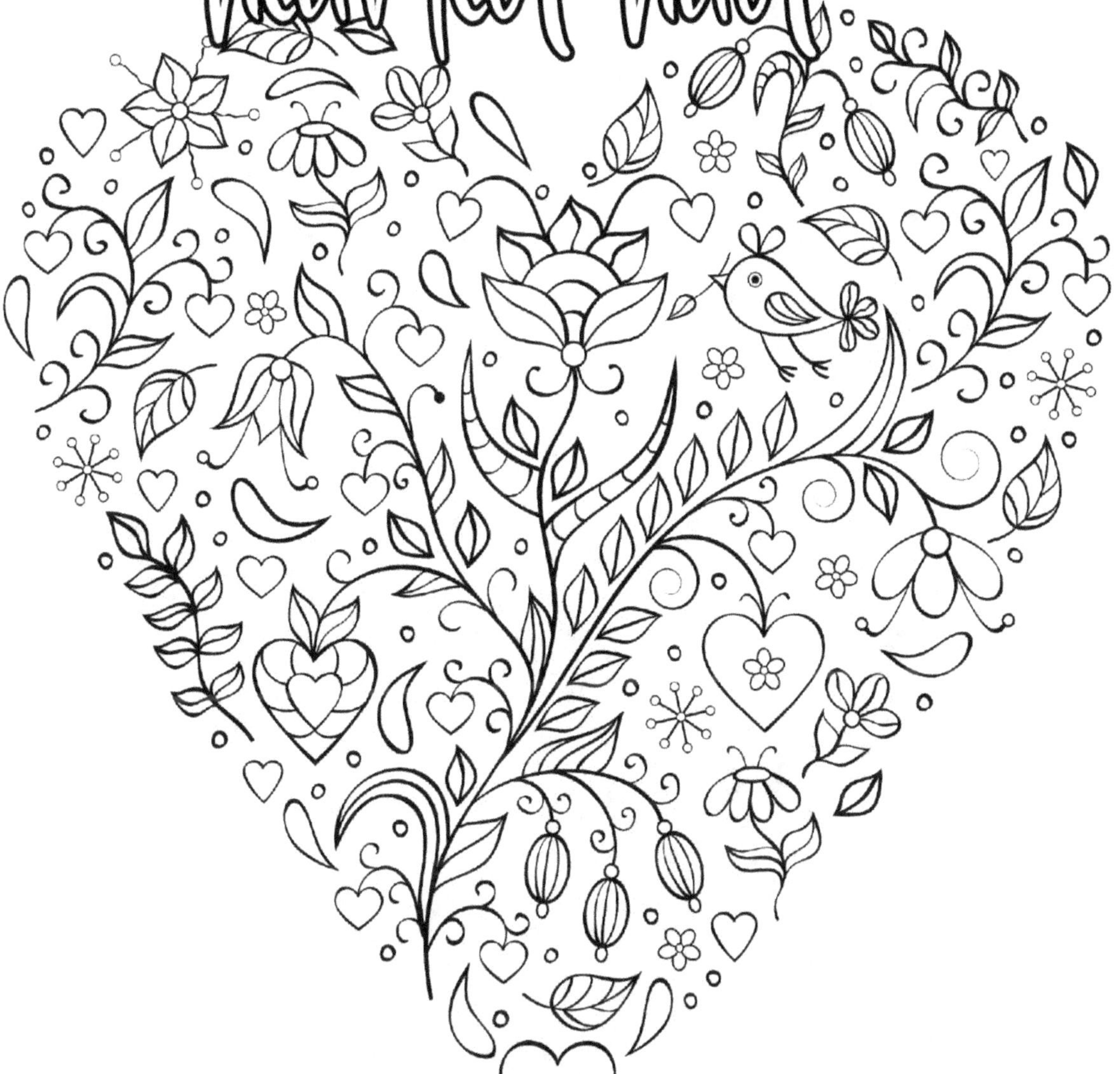

TO POOP BUT

ONLY FARTED

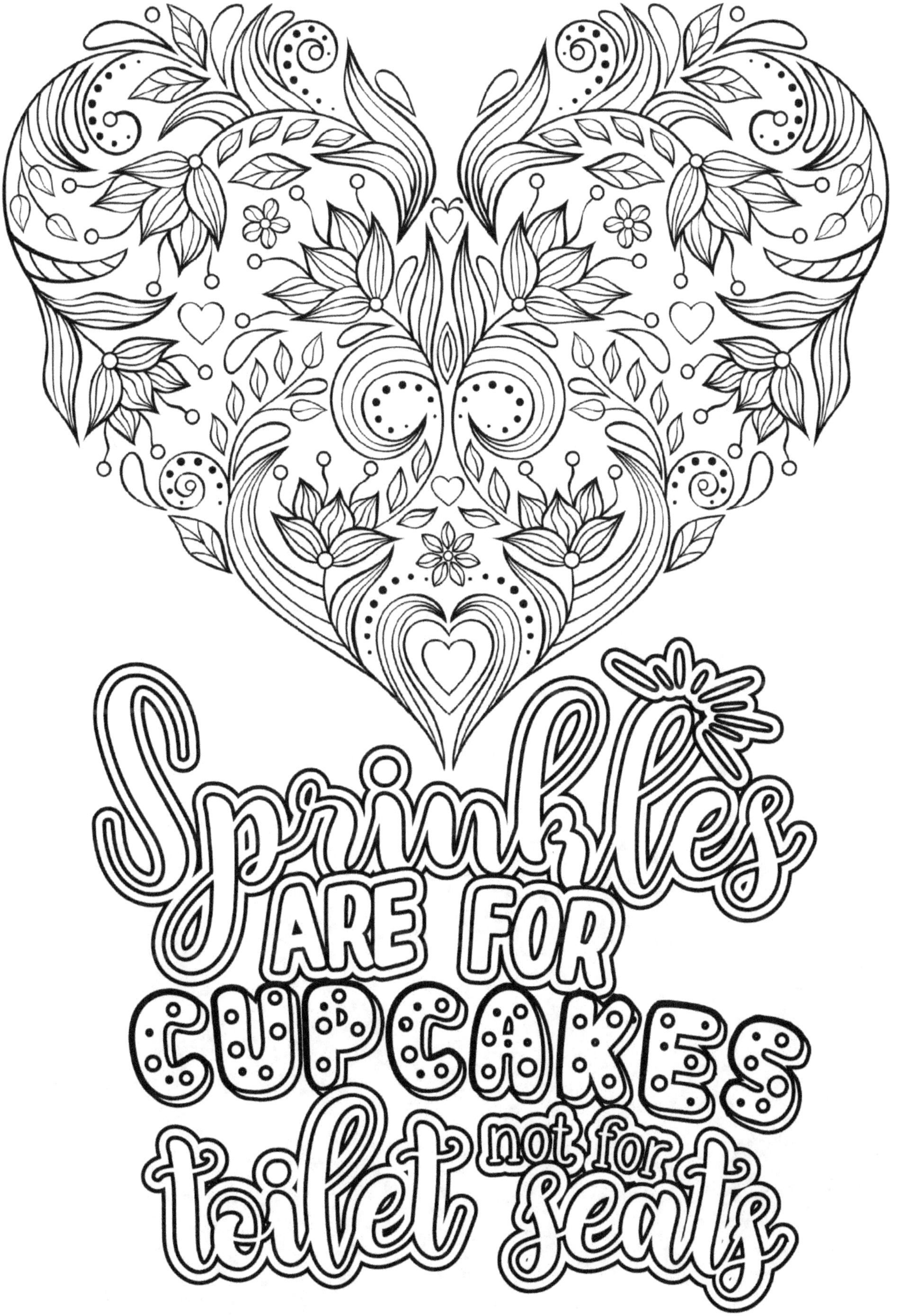

Sprinkles ARE FOR CUPCAKES not for toilet seats

www.ingramcontent.com/pod-product-compliance
Lightning Source LLC
Chambersburg PA
CBHW060437220526
45465CB00008B/3172
* 9 7 9 8 5 9 8 3 6 3 1 8 8 *